DEATH'S SHADOW

OTHER BOOKS BY JON WELLS

Some Kind of Wonderful (with John Ellison) (2012)

Post-Mortem (2009)

Vanished (2009)

Poison (2008)

Sniper (2008)

Heat: A Firefighter's Story (2006)

JON WELLS

DEATH'S SHADOW

True Tales of Homicide

DUNDURN
TORONTO

Project Editor: Michael Carroll
Editor: Dominic Farrell
Design: Courtney Horner
Printer: Webcom

Library and Archives Canada Cataloguing in Publication

Wells, Jon
    Death's shadow : true tales of homicide / by Jon Wells.

 Also issued in electronic format.
ISBN 978-1-4597-0744-3

    1. Murder--Ontario--Hamilton. 2. Murder--Investigation--Ontario--Hamilton. I. Title.

HV6535.C33H35 2012   364.152'30971352   C2012-904609-4

1 2 3 4 5   17 16 15 14 13

Conseil des Arts du Canada   Canada Council for the Arts   Canada   ONTARIO ARTS COUNCIL CONSEIL DES ARTS DE L'ONTARIO

We acknowledge the support of the **Canada Council for the Arts** and the **Ontario Arts Council** for our publishing program. We also acknowledge the financial support of the **Government of Canada** through the **Canada Book Fund** and **Livres Canada Books**, and the **Government of Ontario** through the **Ontario Book Publishing Tax Credit** and the **Ontario Media Development Corporation**.

Care has been taken to trace the ownership of copyright material used in this book. The author and the publisher welcome any information enabling them to rectify any references or credits in subsequent editions.

J. Kirk Howard, President

Printed and bound in Canada.

Visit us at
Dundurn.com
Definingcanada.ca
@dundurnpress
Facebook.com/dundurnpress

Dundurn
3 Church Street, Suite 500
Toronto, Ontario, Canada
M5E 1M2

Gazelle Book Services Limited
White Cross Mills
High Town, Lancaster, England
LA1 4XS

Dundurn
2250 Military Road
Tonawanda, NY
U.S.A. 14150

For my sister Jennifer, with love and appreciation

CONTENTS

ACKNOWLEDGEMENTS

Above all I wish to thank the family members of the victims I write about in this book. They bear infinite burdens of loss, and I thank them for investing their trust in me to tell the stories of their loved ones. I also want to express gratitude toward those members of the Hamilton Police Service who spoke candidly in interviews and provided me with investigation documents, transcripts, and video to assist in my research in both the "Witness" and "Deadly Encounter" stories. Special thanks to Don Forgan, Dave Place, Mike Maloney, Greg Jackson, Peter Abi-Rashed, Annette Huys, Gary Zwicker, Ross Wood, Warren Korol, and Mike Thomas. Thanks to retired detective Don Crath for his indispensable help in my research for the "Eternal Pain" story, and also former Hamilton forensic pathologist Rex Ferris. Police sources were more difficult to access for "Darkness on Indian Trail"; it will become clear why that was. There were law enforcement sources who assisted me, but I cannot name them.

As part of my research, I interviewed three convicted men in person, all of whom are serving time in prison. It offered me a window into their psyches and backgrounds, and also provided me with information on how they committed their crimes. Jailhouse interviews are an intense and disturbing experience. There is no better feeling than seeing a prison in the rear-view mirror when it's over.

Even in today's changing media landscape, there is still such a thing as a robust daily newspaper, and the *Hamilton Spectator* is one. I have been fortunate to work at a place where I have been free to craft long-form narrative stories. At the *Spectator* I want to acknowledge the considerable talents of the photographers whose work appears in this book: Ron Albertson, Barry Gray, John Rennison, and Gary Yokoyama; I would also like to thank my editors and colleagues who assisted on the original version of the stories in *Death's Shadow*: Carla Ammerata, Paul Berton, Agnes Bongers, Tammie Danciu, Jim Poling, Carmelina Prete, and Cheryl Stepan.

I would like to take advantage of this opportunity to thank former editors who have had a big influence on my career: Andy Bader, Chris Clark, Roger Gillespie, Kirk LaPointe, Don Loney, and Dana Robbins.

Thanks to Michael Carroll for welcoming me into the Dundurn fold, and to Dominic Farrell for his copyediting of the book.

Ed Mullen in New York City provided valuable legal counsel in closing the deal on the book contract.

As always, I thank lifelong friends and fellow former Lucas Vikings, Scott Petepiece and Pete Reinjtes.

Finally, I thank my family: the greatest a man could ever hope to have.

PREFACE

In my day job, I write for the *Hamilton Spectator* newspaper. I have grown to love Hamilton, a city that is a study in contradictions. A port city on Lake Ontario, it is a beautiful place, with more than 120 waterfalls and the Niagara Escarpment running through the middle; yet it is still commonly known by its old nickname of Steeltown, and to most outsiders, the image of Hamilton is solely the industrial smokestack view of the town available from the Queen Elizabeth Way highway.

It is a city with a big heart, perhaps the quintessential Canadian city; known, like other Canadian cities, for its low crime rates when compared to similar cities in the United States. But Hamilton has experienced its share of gruesome homicide cases over the years, perhaps owing in part to its status as a border town and in part to the disparity in the socio-economic well-being of its citizens, which is quite significant, depending on which part of the city you live in.

Like the city, the author of this book has, perhaps, his own contradictions. At the *Spectator* I write stories on subjects ranging from the arts to sports and the environment. I have also written eight multi-part narrative series about some of Hamilton's worst crimes and killers. In *Death's Shadow* I have polished and updated four of these stories for publication. All of the pieces, while written in a novelistic style, are true to the last detail; the facts and colour and dialogue are straight from reportage: interviews, documents, and first-hand observation.

I have never covered the police beat and don't really consider myself a crime writer, even though I have now had five true crime books published (arguably six: my first book, *Heat*, is the story of Canada's worst toxic fire, which was set by an arsonist, whom I interviewed). My book *Post-Mortem* was shortlisted for an Arthur Ellis Award for non-fiction crime writing. Perhaps my hesitation to embrace the title of crime writer is simply defensiveness on my part, stemming from the unease I feel writing in such detail about the most unspeakably terrible moments in people's lives, and the killers who created such horror and sadness — and receiving awards for my efforts. (All four stories in *Death's Shadow* have been so honoured.)

Researching and writing about homicide is not something I enter into lightly. Indeed, on occasion I have resisted returning to the genre at all. But at the same time, I have come to the realization that these stories have frequently done some good. They have often highlighted the excellent work of homicide investigators; and I have tried to present full portraits of the victims, which family members have told me has proved comforting. Moreover, the four stories in *Death's Shadow* illustrate that families of victims often must live with incomplete justice, or sometimes no justice at all. I like to think that my stories provide something of a service to the families, and the public, particularly if no suspect was ever arrested and no trial held. That is, they shine a light on the investigation and the victim's story, and the family's grief that everyone in society to some degree should share.

I have also endeavoured to write about such things as courage and love and redemption in these disturbing true stories. The book's title and ominous cover art suggest fear of violent death. But the title is inspired by Psalm 23, often quoted at funerals, in which mourners are invited to try and imagine their loved ones having found a calm and sacred place, even at the end, even at the darkest point: "Yea, though I walk through the valley of the shadow of death, I will fear no evil: for though art with me; thy rod and thy staff they comfort me."

Jon Wells
Hamilton, Ontario

If I ascend into heaven, thou art there: if I make my bed in hell, behold, thou art there. If I take the wings of the morning, and dwell in the uttermost parts of the sea; even there shall thy hand lead me, and thy right hand shall hold me.

— Psalm 139:8–10

Part I

Witness

1

PAINT ON THE WALLS

Father's Day
Sunday, June 18, 2000
Central Police Station
Hamilton, Ontario

The tape rolling, video recorder light blinking, the detective made note of the time: 9:42 p.m. Four hours earlier the witness had been wandering along King Street East downtown. He had been barefoot, wearing a dirty T-shirt — and a diaper. The witness was three years old.

"What's your full name?" the detective asked.

"Eugene."

"Eugene, what's your last name?"

"Charlisa," the boy said. His mother's name.

"Who lives in your house?"

"Pat," he said. Charlisa's boyfriend. "Pat got paint all over the walls."

"Who else lives with Pat?"

"Mama."

"Could you tell me where Pat is?"

"My house."

"What is Pat doing in your house?"

"I dunno. Sleeping in Mama's bed."

"Can you tell me what happened today?"

"Door locked."

"When the door was locked, where were you?"

"With my shoes."

"What did you do when you found the doors locked?"

"Open the lock."

"Then what happened?"

"I opened the doors at my house. Pat's in my house. Pat. All over ... over the wall. Paint all over the walls. Mama's wall."

It had been cool earlier that day and it had rained hard. But the sky had cleared by late afternoon when Eugene entered a variety store on King East. He felt sick. And then, moments later, the boy saw the giant police officer.

The call had come over the police radio at 5:30 p.m. Constable Randy Carter had arranged to end his shift early, planning to get home for the Father's Day barbecue he and his wife were planning with their kids. From what dispatch was telling him, the call — "found child" — would not take long. He'd be home in no time. Carter always shook his head at found-child calls. How could a parent be negligent enough to let a kid go missing in the first place? But the half dozen or so such calls he had handled before had all turned out fine: the child reunited with the parent.

He parked his cruiser in front of K&M Variety and went inside. Carter — hulking size, head shaved bald, silver goatee — saw the child with blond hair in a full diaper that looked ready to burst. A man behind the counter said the boy had thrown up on the floor. Carter greeted the boy, who said nothing. Then he took him outside for air, just as two women came running up the sidewalk. They said the boy's name was Eugene.

"I know where he lives," one of them said.

"Take me there."

They led Carter to an apartment building nearby, went around back, and pointed to the unit on the second floor where the boy lived with his mother. The building was a low rise, the second floor not very high up. Carter climbed the eight metal steps on the outside of the building and knocked at the rear door of unit C. No response. He knocked again, harder.

"Police!"

There was no answer. This was the kind of thing that really grated on him: parents who let their child go missing — and then, what? Head to work? Take a nap? He thumped his big fist on the door again, this time with the intent to force it open. The door opened slightly but was stuck on something; it went no further. He moved back down the stairs. Another tenant showed. She said Eugene's mother's name was Charlisa; said there was a key hanging from the front door of her unit. Things were not going as expected. He knew something was wrong. The barbecue was going to be delayed.

"I'm at 781 King Street East," Carter said into his radio. "Not getting any response from apartment C. Can you send backup?"

He wrote down information from the two women who knew the boy, and left him in their care. Eugene needed clean clothes, a drink, and his temperature taken. Carter moved around to the front of the building, met another officer, and entered.

"We're going in, I need 10-3," he said into his radio, meaning radio silence — no officers speaking on air unless absolutely necessary, keeping the channel clear so he could call for more help. Radio silence was important for another reason: if there was someone inside the premises with bad intentions, he didn't want to advertise that he was coming.

Carter, senses on fire, muscles rigid, expecting to discover something bad, opened the front door to unit C, the keys still dangling from the front lock. He moved through the messy apartment. One of the rooms had art supplies in it, a couple of easels, brushes. He entered the main bedroom. And now he knew. He had gotten hardened on the job. He had been to nasty calls in the past. But nothing like this.

Paint all over the walls.

"Send an ambulance," Carter said. "Make that two."

Eugene, the little blond-haired boy, the first and perhaps only witness at the crime scene, met the detective for questioning later that evening. The detective spent time observing the boy chatting off camera at first. Build rapport, talk about colours, the alphabet, toys, the detective decided. Eugene had good language skills. The detective would start with general questions, then focus.

"Eugene," the detective asked, "who put you to bed last night?"

"Mama. Mama's gone."

"What happened when you woke up?"

"Mama pillow wet. Paint all on Mama pillow."

"What happened when you woke up?"

"Pat's van gone. Man ride it."

"Did you look at this man?"

"Van gone."

"Tell me what happened last night."

"I was sick."

"Did you wake up?"

"Yeah. Mama gone."

"Did you see anyone hurt your mom or Pat?"

"Mom and Pat. They are gone. Mom sleeping, Pat sleeping."

That night forensic identification detectives moved gingerly through the living room of the apartment, the room lit only by the dull glow of the solitary light on the ceiling. *Don't touch anything, not yet.* Hank Thorne was new in ident branch; his partner, Ross Wood, was a veteran at the grisly business. They noted that the door to the balcony, which faced King Street, was wide open. On the balcony, an open purse on a couch. A pair of men's sandals.

Directly beside the living room was the front door to the unit; a key chain hung from the lock. About five paces from the living room, the first room on the left was a tiny bathroom; the light had been left on. Across the hall, on the right, was a child's bedroom: Eugene's room. The overhead light was on, and also the table lamp; the room was messy, toys and clothes all over the floor. The closet door was open.

Three more paces down the narrow hallway, Thorne was writing observations: "Blood noticed on the west wall of the hallway by the light switch, and also on the heating radiator." The door to a second bedroom was open. "Blood on the door frame." Small bedroom, two bodies on the bed, unclothed, male and female. Socks the only clothing on the male; also wearing a gold watch. Fabric anklet on the female; one-inch bruise on the left elbow. Pillow, sheets wet with blood.

Ident officers discovered the murder weapon — a baseball bat — under clothes on the floor of Charlisa's apartment.

Further along from the bedroom, on the right, was a room with art supplies in it, and then the kitchen. On the kitchen floor sat a bucket of dirty water with a mop. The back door was ajar, still partially open since Randy Carter had tried to enter there. The door had been caught on a chain-link lock, which was why it wouldn't open completely before. The apartment was a disaster, littered with clothes. There was lots of work to do on the crime scene: photograph, videotape, label evidence.

In the bedroom the detectives saw it poking out from underneath clothes strewn on the floor.

"Okay. That's interesting," Wood said.

It was the handle of an aluminum baseball bat.

They exited the building and returned with the coroner, noted Thorne.

"Entered master bedroom to pronounce dead."

2

FOREVER YOUNG

Sue Ross had had an odd feeling all that Father's Day afternoon. Something was not quite right. Late that night, asleep in bed, she heard a voice, felt a hand. It was her husband. It was 2:00 a.m.

"You have to get up," he said. "Put on your housecoat."

She walked down the stairs and into the harsh lights of the kitchen. It seemed full of people: strangers in suits, nice clothes, just these … bodies she did not recognize. In fact there were four of them, two men and two women.

"Do you have a daughter named Charlisa?" a voice asked.

It was an uncommon first name, but one that Sue had pegged long before her daughter was born.

Sue had grown up on the water, on the Beach Strip in Hamilton. Her family name was Theroux. As a young girl, she was a star ballet dancer; at Christmas performed in *The Nutcracker* in Montreal; won a scholarship. At the National Ballet School in Toronto, she roomed with a girl from Memphis named Charlisa Lee Cato. Sue loved the name and decided that if she ever had a daughter, that's what she would call the baby.

Sue would eventually marry a man named Al Clark. Al was a risk-taker, loved riding dirt bikes, helicopter skiing. She suggested they do an activity together, take up tennis or something.

"Tennis? You can't get killed doing that," he quipped.

His lifestyle changed dramatically after he broke his neck in a hang-gliding accident. He had been an accomplished glider, but one day crashed into a cliff. He was paralyzed from the neck down.

Their marriage did not last. After they broke up, she stayed single for 20 years, thought about changing her name back to her maiden Theroux, but figured no one could properly pronounce it, much less spell it.

Sue was a strong, plain-talking woman with a dry sense of humour. She was also tough. She had been robbed twice in Hamilton. Once, when she was 28 and working behind the counter of a variety store, a guy wearing a nylon mask pulled a sawed-off shotgun on her. She gave him the money, kept her eyes down, but gave police a decent description of him. They caught him. It was frightening, but she moved on, rolled with it. When Sue finally remarried, she took her new husband's last name: Ross.

When she was still with Al, Sue had her first of two children. On October 15, 1975, Charlisa Lee was born. She later had a son, Greg. Charlisa would ultimately decide to keep her father's last name: Clark. Char, as most came to call her, grew up to be very tall, nearly six feet; she had long hair, big dark eyes. Like her mom she took dance, but her passion and talent lay in art. She would draw on anything she could get her hands on, including her bedroom walls. After high school she left home, eventually had a boy she named Eugene Lee. Her relationship with Eugene's birth father was a stormy one. He was abusive, was convicted for assaulting her. She and Eugene got away, struck out on their own.

On June 1, 1999, when Eugene was two, Charlisa's grandfather — Sue's dad, Camille Theroux — died at 74 from a heart attack. Camille was a great guy, a steamfitter, who had built and driven drag racers. The family was devastated, but took comfort that Camille went the way you're supposed to, without suffering. In his casket at the funeral home, there was a smile on his face. One day Sue would wonder about the timing of it all, her dad going away, suddenly, as though he was needed to comfort a loved one about to enter heaven. At the time she sat down with Eugene and explained what had happened. "Papa became an angel," she told him, "the minute he died."

Charlisa wrote a poem for the funeral. "Raindrops fall and breezes blow but we know in our hearts that he's near," she wrote. "He will watch over us from heaven above and be our guardian angel.... We all will be reunited one day for eternity, and we will always love him, forever young at heart."

Hamilton Spectator

Charlisa and her son Eugene.

Almost a year later, Sue helped Charlisa find a new apartment, at 781 King Street East, unit C, 10 minutes from where Sue lived on Parkdale Avenue. At the back of the apartment, just off the kitchen, Charlisa kept an art room where she painted and where Eugene had his own easel as well. Sometimes she'd go on errands with paint all over her hands. The art room overlooked the back alleyway, fences, and old brick homes; natural light poured in, unlike her bedroom, which was smaller and had no windows.

Charlisa volunteered helping inner city kids, teaching art, cooking for them, mentoring. The girls took to calling her "Mom"; she urged them to get off the street and go back home. Perhaps Charlisa offered that advice because she had left home at a young age herself and had regretted aspects of that decision. As an adult, though, she did enjoy a free-spirited social life. When her mom or 16-year-old brother Greg or her grandmother babysat Eugene, she often would hit a club, a rave, soak up the music, let go.

Her art career had started to bloom, and she thought about pursuing a career as an animator. On June 14, 2000, a painting of Charlisa's was featured at an exhibit in Hamilton called The Power of Healing, and her name was mentioned in the newspaper as one of the artists.

Three days later, on June 17, she spent time with her son, and her boyfriend Pasquale (Pat) Del Sordo. She had known Pat for years, since they had attended high school at Orchard Park, but they had only recently started dating. Eugene got a kick out of Pat; he made him laugh. After spending some time with Charlisa and Eugene, Pat had had to go out, and so, later that night, Charlisa and Eugene were alone. She put the boy to bed, anticipated Pat returning after midnight. It was a warm evening, a night to open the balcony door to let in the breeze.

The next day, June 18, Sue drove with a friend downtown. She had taught ballet for years, and her class was presenting a recital that day. Sue and her friend stopped the car on King East, looked up at Char's low-rise apartment unit, which faced the street, and honked the horn. No one appeared on the balcony, and Sue moved on.

She had been thinking about her daughter a lot lately, was certain that Char was pregnant with her second child. Char had seemed to hint at it to a family member.

"I've got something to tell you, but I don't want to say just yet," Charlisa had said.

At the art show, someone had taken a picture of Charlisa. In the photo her hand rested on her stomach in a motherly pose. She wasn't showing, but Sue believed she could tell; she sensed Char was waiting for the right moment to tell her.

The recital felt odd that afternoon. Usually, Sue was backstage organizing the girls, but this time she sat on a table, let her assistants do the work. She didn't feel like herself. She usually went with her friend for coffee but didn't feel like that today. She just went home.

Now it was the middle of the night, and she was standing in her housecoat, trapped in the repressive light inside her kitchen, in a daze, hearing the voice from one of the bodies ask the question.

"Do you have a daughter named Charlisa?"

"Yes," she said.

"I'm sorry. She's been killed."

Those were the words, Sue thought, but she could never be exactly certain. The words weren't registering; her brain was not able to connect the dots.

She turned to her husband. "What — what are they saying? *What are they saying?*"

Sue bolted from the kitchen, downstairs to the basement where Greg had his bedroom, hysterical, jumping on top of him, slapping at him, screaming, "Char is dead, your sister is dead."

3

COOL INTENSITY

Deep blue eyes meeting dark red; lead homicide detective Don Forgan —
shaved head, wire glasses, suit — examining the walls and bedding in unit C.

"Extremely violent," he said.

The scene was so bloody that some of the initial radio chatter among
the cops suggested that the victims had been shot in the head. But that had
not been the case. There was high-velocity spatter, on the walls, ceiling.
Cast-off patterns. Transfer patterns. Forgan knew the blood patterns well,
having worked in forensic identification with Hamilton Police for 10 years
before transferring to homicide. He saw the male lying face down on the
mattress, the female on the floor, 90 degrees to the bed, arms and head
on the mattress, as though kneeling, her ankles crossed. An odd position.

In his 20 years as a cop, it was not the bloodiest scene he had attended.
No, that had been years before, when he was in uniform. The deceased in
that case was a physician who had severed a major artery and bled out in
large volume, but not before moving through several rooms in his home.
Looked like a homicide; was treated that way at first. But in fact the
doctor had known exactly what he was doing. Suicide.

The crime scene Forgan now examined was disturbing, but then he
had long ago taken to heart advice from a veteran ident man who had
trained him. The person was gone, he was told. It was now just the evidence
left for you. That's all it was. Forgan had tapped that mindset when he had
worked as an investigator in the child-abuse branch. It helped, but then
there was the case of a 14-year-old girl beaten by her father. The father had
used a piece of garden hose. The attacks were so violent that you could see,

Ron Albertson, *Hamilton Spectator.*

Homicide detective Don Forgan.

on the skin of her back, the imprint of the metal coupling of the hose, and even the tiny threads of the coupling. Evidence. Just evidence. But Forgan could not shake that imprint in his mind's eye, even many years later.

In this new case, he knew the little boy, Eugene, had not been hurt, not physically. But the little guy had to have been in the apartment a long time before he made it outside, perhaps 16 hours. What had the boy seen? How would it affect him? Forgan had too big a heart not to feel it.

Don Forgan had started as a cop straight out of high school, bugging an officer at the station until he got hired. He had grown up in Hamilton, the child of Scottish parents. At eight years old, he had been enrolled by his mother in bagpipe lessons. He resisted at first but grew to love the instrument. He eventually played in competitions and won his share. With the pipes you are judged not on the emotion you show while playing, but the emotion conveyed through the tune. Don let it flow through his music.

That was a long time ago. In 1998, after 20 years on the job, he was assigned to homicide, what was then called "the Major Crime Unit." He was made for the work: he was quick-witted and thoughtful, carried a cool intensity, was always up for a case. He could put a family in pain at ease in the morning and grill a suspect in the afternoon with equal effectiveness.

On his first day on the job in homicide, January 4, 1998, he was assigned to partner with Warren Korol, who was riding high in the branch, having arrested Stoney Creek serial poisoner Sukhwinder Dhillon three months earlier after chasing the case all the way to India. Forgan walked in the door on the second floor at Central Station and Korol met him immediately.

"Don't bother taking your coat off, Donny; we've gotta head out. New case."

"But I don't even know where the coffee machine is yet."

The case was a missing person/suspected homicide; the victim's name Sheryl Sheppard. The body was missing, so there was no crime scene. They started at her apartment. Rule number one: always start at the victim; start with people closest to her, and work out.

It was now more than two years ago that Forgan had started in homicide and he had tackled many investigations since, but as he cracked the new case notebook for the double murder, that first case, while still open, had gone nowhere. He remained frustrated that someone was walking around free out there who should be locked up.

In the bedroom of the apartment on King East, Forgan saw a mark on the floor: a tread from an athletic shoe, a print left in blood. And there was the baseball bat. Ident had removed the clothing that had partially covered it. Blood was visible on the fat part of the bat. The killer did not bring it to the scene; a neighbour told police that she had loaned Charlisa the bat to use for protection. Char always kept it by the front door. It was a weapon of opportunity. If it was the murder weapon, why did the killer leave it behind? Maybe he rifled through drawers looking for money, tossed clothes around, and accidentally covered the bat? How could he forget to get rid of it? Forgan wondered. But then who knew what your thought process was like after you've killed two people, Forgan reflected. Media would soon be on the story full bore. They would need to keep the bat a secret as holdback evidence. Only one person out there knows about the bat.

Police had started interviewing neighbours; no one had heard anything unusual coming from that apartment. Forgan exited the bedroom, walked up the narrow hallway to the living room, where the open door led on to the balcony. He chatted with Korol, who had joined him at the scene. They could hear voices in an adjoining unit, so the detectives spoke quietly. If the walls were that thin, how could no one have heard anything, with the violence that had happened here? Forgan listened to the old hardwood floor under his feet creak. Did the victims hear the guy coming?

He knew the investigation would be complicated. Two victims — two circles of friends and relatives and acquaintances and potential enemies and motives. The only witness so far was the kid, who was speaking in riddles. No sign of forced entry to the apartment. Did the victims, or at least one of them, know the killer?

Forgan left the living room and walked out the front door of the unit, saw the key chain dangling from the lock. It was the mother's key chain. Who left it there? It would make no sense for the killer to lock the door and leave the key on his way out, unless he was trying to throw them off. The kid? The boy clearly had not exited via the chain-locked back door; more likely he had exited through the front, and then locked the door like he had seen his mother do many times before.

Forgan walked down a flight of stairs and out into the darkness, to the strip of grass in front of the apartment building. Shoe indentations on the grass. On the front concrete facade, the word *Victoria* and an iron lamp fixture below the balcony of unit C. The second-floor balcony was maybe 10 feet off the ground. Someone with strength and purpose could grab the fixture, climb up to the balcony, and hop back down again. Might explain the pronounced footprints in the grass.

His night ended at 4:00 a.m. Forgan drove home, caught a few hours' sleep, and was back in the office at Central Station Monday at 9:30 a.m. He had three voice mails from reporters about the case already. That afternoon he attended autopsies for both victims performed by forensic pathologist Dr. Chitra Rao. Her conclusion: both were bludgeoned to death; struck numerous times in the head and face. Multiple skull fractures and hemorrhages in the brain. Tramline bruising caused by striking by a cylindrical object. Later that day Forgan drove to Stoney Creek with Detective Dave Place, who had been among those called in to assist. The second of the victims, the male, had been identified by fingerprints. The family had to be notified.

4

"I'M GOING TO BE OKAY"

It had been a sad year for Ruth Del Sordo. She had lost her mother, Lily, in February. Ruth's husband had tried to tell her all the right things, that Lily had lived a good and long life, 84 years. But Ruth had been very close with her mother, could not believe she was gone. Lily had family who were killed by the Nazis during the Second World War, but her parents made it to England, where she was born. The family moved to Canada after the war, and ended up in Hamilton, where Lily raised a family on her own after her husband left her. Ruth grew up on the Beach Strip, went to Van Wagners Beach School on the lake, the building that would one day be reborn as Barangas restaurant. She married an Italian-Canadian named Flavio Del Sordo in 1973.

Their first child, Pasquale, was born a year later, on September 20, 1974. Ruth and Flavio had four other kids: Anthony, Flavio Jr., Cindy, and Joey. Flavio started a construction company; all the boys worked for him.

Pasquale especially loved the work, had a passion for woodworking since he picked up a toy hammer as a toddler. In his teens he won awards for woodworking and carpentry projects. As the first-born, he occupied a special place in the family, but especially in Ruth's world. He had had epilepsy as a boy, but with treatment his symptoms had vanished before he hit his teens. Still, Ruth had never stopped worrying about Pasquale, even into his twenties. They continued to be very close. He shared everything with her, and was always driving her places, taking her shopping. Ruth always got a steady dose of the music he cranked in the house or car. He used to always give her a big hug, and say, "Me and you against the world, eh, Mom?"

Pasquale "Pat" Del Sordo.

She was fiercely protective of him; one of his girlfriends once broke up with him because he paid so much attention to his mother. When he was in his early twenties, Pasquale and a girlfriend had a child, a girl. They did not stay together, though. Still, Ruth glowed with pride when, in the early days, she saw him bathe and diaper the baby.

By the summer of 2000, nearing his 26th birthday, Pasquale, who now went by the name his friends had given him, Pat, worked for his dad framing houses and still lived upstairs in the family home in Stoney Creek. He loved to go out at night, though. He loved his food and music; fixing up his blue Jeep and riding around blasting classic Kiss; heading out at night with six or seven of his fingers adorned with gold rings; taking centre stage on the dance floor at clubs, all 5 foot 11, 240 pounds of him. Others gravitated toward him, his big laugh and brassy presence.

His dad warned him not to stay out too late. Pat often had to work early in the morning, and most of all he needed to be careful out there. But Pat seemed to trust everyone. "Don't worry, I'm going to be okay," he said, and gave Flavio a hug and playfully pinched his cheek.

Even when he had a late night, Pat always returned home to sleep in his own bed. That continued during the summer of 2000, when he was seeing Charlisa Clark. Saturday afternoon, June 17, he hung with Charlisa and her son, Eugene, and then, later that night, he was out with his friends Moe and Luca in Burlington at a carnival on the lakeshore. They stopped at a club called Billy Bob's, but the lineup was too big, so they decided to pack it in. Pat was dropped off at the Del Sordo home just after midnight.

His family had plans for Sunday, Father's Day: everyone was going to the Mandarin for a big dinner, as was the custom. Soon after midnight, Charlisa called him on his cell. He left the house, took his dad's white Del Sordo Construction van and drove the 15 minutes to visit Charlisa at her apartment on King Street East; parked in a lot right across the street.

Ruth woke up at 9:00 a.m. on Sunday. Pat had not come home. She was worried, and called his cell repeatedly. No answer, just his voice mail. At 4:45 p.m. Ruth and Flavio drove downtown to pick up their youngest, Joey, from where he was getting off a shift working at Tim Hortons. On the way, driving along King East, they noticed the white van in a parking lot. They did not know that Charlisa lived across the street. Flavio phoned his son Anthony; told him to bring the extra set of keys. Flavio opened the back door of the van, which was unlocked. Anthony left his father, and Flavio drove the van home by himself.

It was 7:00 p.m. and no one had heard from Pat yet. The family decided to go back to the spot on King Street where the van had been parked. Flavio, Anthony and his fiancée, Joey, and Pat's friends Luca and Moe went down. The area near 781 King Street East now buzzed with police; yellow crime-scene tape was up. Did it have anything to do with Pat? Officers asked them to come to Central Station, where detectives began interviewing Pat's family and friends. Did anyone have any reason to harm Pat? Had he had any trouble with friends or girlfriends? Any drug use? No, the family replied, everyone loved Pat; he didn't take drugs and was hard on people who did, even if they just smoked cigarettes.

Flavio phoned Ruth, who was still at home. "I don't know what's going on," he said. "The police are saying there are two people found dead in an apartment on King Street, but are not saying who it is."

Ruth dropped the phone, fearing the worst.

"Please!" she yelled, "Don't take my Pasquale! Take me! God, take me!"

All that night, still uncertain if her son was alive, Ruth prayed, asked God for a miracle, even as she sensed the truth. Flavio suggested maybe Pat had been in a fight, was attacked, had fled town?

No, Ruth thought, *he would have come home, no matter what*. Her Pasquale always came home. She kept thinking back to the night before, the last time he had been in the house. Ruth had heard Pat leave to go see Charlisa. She had wanted to stop him. But Flavio had recently given her a hard time about being so protective of their son. "Don't phone him all the time; he's a man," he had said.

When Ruth asked Pat about the argument she had had with Flavio, however, he said, "Don't ever stop bugging me, Ma; it just shows you love me."

That night, when he had just left for Charlisa's, Ruth had had a mind to call him on his cell: "It's too late, Pasqua, tomorrow's Father's Day — come on back; we'll have some coffee, talk a bit." Ruth knew if she had called that he would have come back. No question about it. How many times had he cancelled dates in the past if she needed him? Many times. But no, she had not called him. Why? Why hadn't she just called him once more, kept him home where he belonged?

Just after 5:00 p.m. Monday, Don Forgan and Dave Place pulled in in front of the Del Sordo home, the house the family had renovated. Pat himself had helped screw down every new floor. Just 15 hours earlier, Dave Place had stood in Sue Ross's kitchen to pass along the news of Charlisa's death. And now he was doing it again. Place dreaded such notifications, personally bearing the worst news in a family's life, a dark moment of the soul they would never forget.

The detectives were invited inside. They told the Del Sordos one of the victims in the apartment on King Street East was Pat. Some sat in silence. Pat's brother Anthony punched a pane of glass in the china cabinet, slicing a tendon in his hand. The family wrapped it and rushed him to hospital. Ruth just sat there, absorbing the news, her heart shattered. *My boy is gone*, she thought. *My music man. My Pasquale.*

Pat's cell phone was recovered from the apartment. Detectives monitored it, waiting to see if anyone called in the days that followed. There was one person who dialed the number several times. It was Ruth. She yearned to hear his voice on the recording, the one that said without fail, "Hello, this is The Pasqua — if you got something hot or interesting to say, just leave a message after the beep. Ciao."

Ruth focused her energy on the investigation, her sorrow competing with puzzlement and anger. Her boy was gentle, full of fun. Who could want to harm him? Moreover, she could not fathom it — he was a large man, with big arms and shoulders, muscled from weight lifting and building houses; a gentle giant but so strong he could kill a man with a punch. Who could possibly have done this to him, she wondered? Surely not just one man.

5

COLD BLOODED

After it had all gone down, Carl crashed at a friend's apartment. In the morning he rose, stood on the balcony high in the sky, thought about what he had done, what he had seen and heard. *Jump? Should he?* The thought crossed his mind, and not for the first time. Except Carl had issues with suicide. Not that he considered himself religious, but, still, he wondered: *What if it was true that you burned in hell for it? On the other hand, what if, when you die, everything was just black?* That would be good; he would choose suicide if that were the case.

Mostly, he wondered if he had cleaned up enough back at the apartment. So much blood. After it was over, he had hopped off the low-rise balcony of the apartment on King East to escape. But then he had returned, scaled the wall again, through the open balcony door, and wiped down everything: walls, light switches. What had he touched? Anything that would stick? He hopped off the balcony again, threw one of his shoes in a dumpster, another in a second dumpster. Then he returned to the apartment a final time, remembering he had handled a wallet in there. Grabbed the wallet, a set of car keys, left; threw it all down a sewer.

The next day he visited his girlfriend, Elaine, who lived down at Melvin and Parkdale in the east end, six kilometres away from where it had happened on King Street. They had a stormy relationship; his violent temper and drug habit did not help. She once called police to complain that Carl had stolen her VCR.

Ron Albertson, *Hamilton Spectator*.

Carl Hall climbed the outside wall of the apartment before killing Charlisa and Pat.

Carl turned on her TV and asked her what channel the Hamilton news was on. That was odd, she thought. He never watched the news. He saw a journalist on the screen, reporting from the scene outside the apartment on King East. The journalist was talking about a double homicide.

Elaine looked at Carl. "What? Did you have something to do with that?" Elaine asked.

"No."

In the past, when they were high, they had talked about what violence each might be capable of doing.

"I believe in God," Elaine had said. "I couldn't kill anyone."

Carl sat there, with his red hair, bloodless white skin, pale blue-grey eyes that seemed to possess a crazed light, an unhinged quality. As a teenager growing up back east, in the Maritimes, Carl had once dreamed of killing someone. Woke up thinking it had actually happened. No, it wouldn't bother him, killing, he told Elaine. "Because I don't have a conscience."

He left Elaine's place and headed again for the apartment on King Street East. The Hamilton Police command van was there; there were uniform and plain clothes cops, news reporters.

Why did he return to the scene? To see what they might have on him? That's what he told one person. Or was there another reason? Why would he risk showing his face there, outside the place where he had killed two people in cold blood, uncertain if anyone had spotted him? For that matter, why did he drop hints to Elaine about what he had done? Maybe his behaviour was explained by something very dark that beat inside him.

He moved closer to the yellow police crime scene tape, his thoughts spinning.

"Hey, stay back," ordered a cop in uniform.

"Okay."

One day, down the road, Carl would reflect about having taken two lives. He had done something that most people didn't get to do. *Didn't get to do? An odd statement to make*, he thought. He knew that.

A couple of weeks before the double murder, a man fought through tears for the right words, as a north wind off the Bay of Fundy whipped his face, along with a hard rain. Shane Mosher was 32, thin, with a boyish face and short dark hair. He lived in Brantford, Ontario, 30 minutes west of Hamilton, but had travelled to his boyhood home of Middleton, a small town in Nova Scotia's Annapolis Valley, to see his mom, Barb. She was dying of colon cancer and time was running out. It was tearing him apart.

Mom was an angel of a woman, had always been there for him. When he was a boy growing up in the valley, however, Shane's relationship with his father had been more complicated. He wanted to emulate his dad, or some of him, anyway. He didn't want his day job, that was for sure. Dad worked at a funeral home next door to their house. He was an embalmer. Shane always stayed away from the basement of the place; it freaked him out. But there were other things about his dad that Shane admired. His dad had been a great athlete, a local legend; he had played for Canada's national baseball team, the one that toured Cuba and met Fidel Castro in 1964. Shane kept a scrapbook of the pictures. Dad was a good looking guy; women loved him; guys wanted to be like him. But Shane came to believe that his dad struggled to deal with life, with not living up to the shadow of his own father, and not making it big-time in sports.

Visiting his mom for what he knew would be the last time, Shane was nervous. His mind was racing. What should he say? He came to the front door of her house, where she was receiving palliative care. Shane had come down with a sore throat and earache, which he had mentioned to his stepfather. The stepfather wouldn't let him in the door because of his symptoms. Shane pleaded with him; it was the last time he would see her. *Please.* The stepfather said no. Instead he set Barb up in a room at the front of the house, by a window. Shane had had to stand outside in the wind and rain, talk to her through a screen, both of them crying. She died on June 13 at 52 years old.

That summer, back home in Brantford, Shane continued his life with Shannon, his wife, and their one-year-old girl, Riley. On the outside he was still good ol' Shane from the valley: likable, clean-cut, big smile. But inside everything was a struggle; he could not shake the sadness. He talked to a doctor about it. Was he losing it, going crazy? Shane reflected on his own history a lot — such an unusual life, he reflected: how he grew up back east; how he had taken it on the chin more than a few times but kept on surviving.

He had always yearned for a solid family life, but his parents had broken up when he was young. Sports had filled the void: he was a ranked tennis player and a standout baseball player; led his team to the Eastern Canadian championships after making a game-winning catch over the outfield fence. Strong hockey player, too. But it seemed to Shane that whenever he looked up into the stands, his dad was never there; he was hanging with his buddies having beers instead.

There were some tough times. There was the time when Shane was 16, when he had caught a ride hitchhiking. The driver was a sexual predator; had tried to make a move on him. As the car slowed around a bend, Shane opened the door, jumped out, and got away. And then, at 21, he was in a bad car accident. Shane's best friend, Dave, who was driving, died when their pickup truck crashed through a guardrail and plunged 100 feet down a hill. Shane didn't have his seatbelt on, had been sleeping, but somehow emerged with just a cut.

When he met Shannon, she was coming off a bad marriage. Shane was attracted immediately to the popular, blonde — she was a pretty woman with a big personality. Shane felt like he had won the lottery when they started dating. After marrying they had Riley.

That was a few years ago, though; now, back in Brantford, after his mom died, he was drinking some, smoking pot a bit, which he had done on occasion in his valley days, when he'd have a joint and a beer with the guys after hockey. But it wasn't enough, not anymore. He could not clear his head, shake his depression, and could not bring himself to talk to Shannon about it. He was acting outside his own skin now. Shane Mosher was about to plunge into another world, put everything at risk, and head down a road where he would find himself face to face with a killer and a fateful decision.

6

"DID YOU KILL CHAR?"

The night police told her about Charlisa, Sue Ross turned her thoughts almost immediately to her grandson, Eugene. He had to have been in the apartment when Char was killed.

"What about Eugene?" she asked. "Where is he?"

The police officers told her that he was fine, unhurt. He had been interviewed once by police, was with social services.

"Well, he has to be with me," she said.

After taking heart that Eugene was unharmed, Sue next felt fear that Eugene's birth father, who had been long estranged from Charlisa, would make a move for custody. Sue could not let that happen. The man had been abusive toward her daughter and had a criminal record.

The day after she was informed of the murder, Sue was reunited with Eugene. She needed to convey to her grandson that his mother was gone. Sue had once told him that his grandfather became an angel when he died. She took the same approach. She sat him on her knee.

"Your mommy, Charlisa, is an angel now," she said. "Just like Papa."

Hearing the words, Eugene sat straight up, rigid.

"No, she's not," he said.

Sue spoke very quietly, but firmly. He had to know. "Yes, she is," she said.

She took Eugene to meet the police for a second interview, this time with a Hamilton detective named Duncan McCulloch.

"What happened when you went to sleep?" he asked the three-year-old.

"My mama gone."

"Mama put you to sleep?"

"Yeah."

"Was anyone else there?"

"Pat."

"When you went to sleep, who else was in the apartment?"

"Pat's friend."

"Who's Pat's friend?"

"Got paint ... all over ... Pat. Paint all over."

"We'll slow down. When you woke up, what happened?"

"Me."

"Was it light out or dark?"

"Light."

"Who else was with you?"

"Me."

"Anyone else?"

"Pat."

"Where's Pat?"

"In bed, my house, in mama's bed."

"Where was mama?"

"I dunno. She was gone."

"Were you lonely for a long time?"

"Yeah."

"What did you do?"

"TV broken. Cord gone."

"How did you get out?"

"Me."

"How did you open the door, was it heavy?"

"Yes. Big door."

Eugene's words during the course of two interviews had not been easy to decipher, but a picture emerged: he had tried to wake his mother and Pat; had seen the blood-soaked bedding and walls — blood he equated, given Charlisa's passion for art, with paint. He tried to watch TV but it was broken, perhaps disabled by the killer, if the TV had been working at all before. He had been "with his shoes," perhaps hiding in his closet, either during the murders or after. He talked of seeing someone drive a white van away outside the building. That had been Pat's father, Flavio Del Sordo.

The detective mentioned a new name to the boy.

"Do you know Spencer?"

"Yes."

"Who's Spencer?"

"Pat's friend."

"Was he there with you?"

"No."

"When you were alone in the apartment, was Spencer there?"

"Yeah."

"What did he say?"

"Mama gone."

"Who told you Mama's gone?"

"Me. Couldn't find her. Hiding."

"You couldn't find her?"

"No."

Spencer was among those individuals Charlisa had known well, someone that Lead Detective Don Forgan was working to eliminate as a suspect in the early hours of the investigation. There had been no forced entry to the apartment, so it seemed possible that the killer knew at least one of the victims. Those who kill often do so for love or money. Charlisa had no money. Could it have been a jealous ex-boyfriend? She had previously had a relationship with Spencer, who worked at a club she frequented. A friend of Charlisa's said she had once been "crazy about him."

On June 21 Forgan interviewed Spencer at the man's home in Hamilton. He told Forgan he had known Char for several years, and said that they had dated on and off. He had last spoken with her just two days before she was murdered. It was an interesting admission, but then the man also co-operated enthusiastically with Forgan — offered a blood sample for DNA, his palm print, finger print, two pairs of shoes, and his watch for examination. That same afternoon, he volunteered to take a lie-detector test.

"Last weekend," the polygraph officer asked him, "did you kill Char?"

"No."

"Last weekend, was it you who killed Char?"

"No."

"Last weekend, were you the person who killed Char?"

"No."

The officer said Spencer's physiological reactions indicated that he was telling the truth. And, ultimately, forensics, including shoe prints found at the scene, did not match his. He was cleared.

Forgan continued eliminating associates of Charlisa and Pat's from consideration as suspects. Start the circle tight, work from the victim out, and that includes the families. Forgan investigated Charlisa's abusive ex, Eugene's father. The man worked as a bouncer at a bar in Lindsay, two hours northeast of Hamilton, near Peterborough. Forgan called the Lindsay police and asked them to pay the man a visit. Police officers showed at his door and asked where he was the night of the murders. He told them that he had been working at the bar until closing time, then he had hung with co-workers until very late, arrived at his home where he lived with his mother. He added that he did not own a car. He said he hadn't seen Charlisa for two years. Not only would he never hurt her, he said, but he actually had people in Hamilton keeping an eye out for her.

"I still have love for the lady," he told the officers. He asked how his son was doing.

Don Forgan needed to take the guy's measure himself. He drove up to Lindsay, entered the darkened tavern in mid-afternoon, wearing a suit as usual. A group of regulars huddled at the bar. They all went silent. Forgan felt a smile. Could they tell he was from out of town?

"Is the manager around?" Forgan asked pleasantly.

He interviewed Charlisa's ex, who repeated what he had told the Lindsay police: he had been at the bar the night of the murders until 5:00 a.m. He went straight home, had coffee with his mother. Forgan interviewed the other employees at the bar, who all confirmed that he had worked till close and that they left with him. He gave Forgan his fingerprints and palm prints, and readily agreed to take a polygraph. But when he took the test, the results suggested he was being deceptive. He grew angry when hearing the result, but insisted he was innocent.

Forgan knew that his alibi seemed solid. The man did not have opportunity to come to Hamilton in the window when the murders took place. But was the guy beyond arranging for someone else to do it? In Forgan's book that remained an open question.

At the same time, the detective worked to eliminate other individuals, including members of Pat Del Sordo's family, such as Pat's father. Flavio had been alone in the white Del Sordo construction van, the one Pat had driven to Charlisa's. The afternoon after the murder, Flavio was the one who drove it back home from the scene. Why did he do that? The van was needed for the investigation and had been towed to the police station for examination.

Forgan asked Flavio to supply shoe, finger, and palm prints, and take a polygraph. Pat's father provided prints, but bristled at doing a polygraph. Pat's mom, Ruth, grew frustrated with the investigation, and told the police so. Their son, her Pasquale, had been murdered; they were beyond grief, and, yet, the detectives kept questioning their family. It was too much to bear. Flavio would die for his son, and Pat worshipped his father, she said. But since Flavio did not want to take the polygraph, it kept him in the investigative loop.

Down the road in the investigation, Ruth, at the end of her rope, volunteered to take the lie detector test instead. When the polygraph officer asked her about any potential involvement of her husband, she laughed. "Not in a million years," she said.

In the apartment the ident team found traces of blood in the bathroom on a hand towel, a diluted drop on the edge of the tub, and another on the sink's hot water tap. The killer had tried to clean up. Did he leave fingerprints? The Ontario Provincial Police (OPP) were called in to assist with their forensic laser truck. Wearing orange goggles OPP investigator Dave Sibley joined Hamilton detectives Hank Thorne and Ross Wood, scanning the apartment for fingerprints with a blue-green laser projected from a fibre-optic cable. If the laser detected a print, it would stand out. But this time it revealed no fingerprints on any of the walls or doors inside the apartment. The result was disappointing but not shocking: most people don't leave fingerprints in everyday life.

Identifiable prints are deposited if sufficient pressure is applied to a surface, and if the digit has secreted natural substances (sweat, lipids) or transferred foreign substances (blood).

Next, they sprayed surfaces in the apartment with chemicals such as leuchocrystal violet, to reveal more signs of blood. After spraying the floors, small footprints appeared in purple — Eugene's footprints. He had trailed blood to the kitchen and living room, back and forth, around the apartment after the murders, the footprints fading as the blood wore off his bare feet.

Sibley took several items back to his lab for testing: bottles, glasses — and the aluminum baseball bat. Hank Thorne explored the shoe tread impression left in blood on the bedroom floor. Don Forgan had people of interest submit shoes for examination — including officers who first reported to the scene — so Thorne could check for a match. The impression appeared to be from a Reebok running shoe — identifiable because of the distinctive intersecting-lines pattern. Thorne visited local stores looking for a tread-design match in Reebok shoes but had no luck. He went to Reebok Canada and pored through catalogues. It became apparent the shoe was probably not a Reebok, but a knock-off.

On June 23, at 8:00 a.m., Dave Sibley examined the rubber grip of the baseball bat for prints in his OPP lab. The standard procedure was to start with the least invasive method, then, if necessary, apply chemicals to draw out a print. Sibley sat in a dark room with a lamp box that projected a concentrated white light. He shone it on the grip, the light turning the black rubber a milky colour. There: ridge detail. It was a palm print, made in some kind of residue: a substrate, perhaps sweat. Had to be from the killer's hand. He felt a rush, got his camera and took photos of the print, then phoned Hank Thorne with the news. It was a big break. They needed another: a palm print to match it.

Hamilton police stored fingerprints in an electronic database for easy scanning and comparison, but the same was not true for palm prints. Assuming Charlisa and Pat's killer happened to have a palm print on file in Hamilton, it would be among all those collected over the years, taken from suspects arrested for break and enters and robberies. Those palm prints were on cards filed away by name in a box — about 3,000 of them. "Like looking for a needle in a stack of needles," said Thorne.

7

BAD MAN

Carl wondered if the police might come after him, but as the weeks and months passed, he felt safer. At times he thought back to that night, to the blood, the sounds. He remembered feeling that night like he was outside himself, looking at what was going down. The girl's death: that bothered him, because she had a little boy. Carl saw the boy in the other room. Had to be her kid. But the guy, the big guy, he didn't feel so much for him.

He was no multiple murderer, he thought, not some sick guy. On the other hand, while Carl wasn't much for self-examination, he did wonder if, maybe, with his temper, and the violence he had displayed over the years against men and women, he was bad inside. Evil. He didn't blame his behaviour on his upbringing.

Carl was born November 26, 1974, in Hamilton. His family had moved back and forth between Sussex, New Brunswick, where they had roots, and Hamilton. Mostly, Carl grew up out east. He was never sure why they kept moving; the family history always seemed a bit shady to him, more than a little screwed up. He had one sibling, Audrey, who shared his red hair, but they had little else in common. When Audrey was 16, she decided to leave home out east. Carl came home one day to find she had suitcases packed in the hallway.

"Well?" she said. "See the suitcases? Want to say anything about that?"

"No," Carl said.

"I'm leaving."

"Good luck."

And that was it. She ran away to a relative in Hamilton, eventually settled out west.

Carl didn't have many friends growing up; had girlfriends, but not guys. He had a bad relationship with his father. One day, when he was 13, he was out hunting in the bush. His father had walked ahead up on a knoll. Carl fell in behind. He was freezing cold, shivering. He took off the safety on his 20-gauge shotgun and sighted on the back of his dad's head, finger on the trigger. A couple of positive images popped into his mind. His mom. His dog. He lowered the shotgun and put the safety back on.

He felt like he stood up to his dad for the first time, face to face, when he was 15. Carl was smoking a lot of pot, and one day he was doped up and walked up to his old man, jutted his chin out, and challenged him. He knew he saw fear in the man's eyes.

At 18, Carl was convicted for a break and enter and assault. After that he moved out west: Edmonton. He began smoking lots of hash; fled town with outstanding drug possession and break and enter charges. He returned to Hamilton and dated a woman named Tracy. He ripped her off, withdrew $1,000 from her bank account, and left town, hitchhiking to New Brunswick. Carl later returned to Hamilton and got back together with Tracy and they had a daughter. The relationship didn't last. The final straw was a fight in December 1997. Carl had finished cooking steaks. Something set him off and he threw the food in the garbage in a rage. Tracy slapped him in the head.

"Stop, or I'll hurt you," he said, and then hit her to the ground.

He was convicted for assault in January. Police shipped him back to Edmonton to answer the charges he had fled there. He served eight months in jail then returned to Hamilton.

A restraining order kept him from Tracy and his daughter. He and a buddy, who had a car, would pull in front of Tracy's house, burn rubber, crank tunes. It bothered Carl, not being able to see his daughter. He fumed that Tracy was being a cold bitch.

It was in 1999 that he experienced an awakening. Carl was dating a stripper, trying to make Tracy jealous. The stripper introduced him to crack. He inhaled, held it in, exhaled. She started to speak. He grinned, raised his hand. "Shhh — quiet for second," he said. "You know what? That's what I've been looking for all my life."

For Carl it was a new beginning and a dark end. The violent fire that had burned inside him for as long as he could remember now had new fuel. He was hooked. He spent every dollar he made, and stole, on crack.

In the summer of 2000, he was cracking it up a lot. The Father's Day weekend was not a good time for Carl, not with his memories of his own dad and the restraining order keeping him from his own child. He needed an escape. He needed some cash.

He saw an open door on the balcony of the apartment on King East. A bat leaning by the front door. Down the hallway, past the kid's room. Big guy on the bed. Blood. More blood, and the sound of final breaths. That sound — Carl couldn't take it. He had to make it stop. *Stop breathing*, he thought. A young woman appeared. He knew what he had to do.

In the fall the investigation was into its third month and detective Don Forgan was nowhere close to making an arrest. On September 27 he spoke with a child life specialist at McMaster University in Hamilton, who agreed to engage little Eugene in play therapy, study his actions and words.

"Did mommy get hurt a little or a lot?" she asked him.

"Lots."

"Did you see who hurt mommy?"

"Yes."

"Were there one, two, or three people?" she asked, holding up three fingers.

Eugene held up three fingers in response. Did that mean two victims and one killer? Or had there been more than one attacker?

Sue Ross attended the play therapy sessions and took notes. At one point Eugene was given a dollhouse to play with, including figures of a man, a woman, and a baby. He smashed the dolls, put the baby in a car, and drove it away. It appeared as though he was re-creating what had happened to him. One day he asked the therapist for markers. He took a red marker and marked up the inside of the dollhouse, red splashed everywhere.

How close had Eugene come to the killer that night? Eventually, in therapy, he said that the "bad man has scary eyes."

Forgan believed that Eugene had been eye-to-eye with the killer, perhaps while hiding in his closet. The therapy was meant to encourage Eugene to recall any information that might be useful to the investigation, and also to help him deal with his mother's death. That transition had been a painful one. He was now terrified of the dark, could not get to sleep, and cried often. Sue kept him in her bed every night.

To help Eugene complete the circle of what happened to him on Father's Day, Constable Randy Carter came to Eugene's home, saw the boy for the first time since meeting him at the variety store on King Street East that day. Carter now gave him a teddy bear. Eugene christened it "Police Bear," and slept with it every night.

Meanwhile, Forgan chased every angle. He sought help from veteran OPP criminal profiler Jim Van Allen. In December Van Allen offered his analysis. No forced entry to the apartment, victims naked on the bed, the child unharmed: it suggested to Van Allen that the primary target had been Charlisa, and it was probable that a lone killer was responsible — one who had a previous intimate relationship with her.

On January 3, 2001, Forgan met Charlisa's son for the first time. He had studied notes from Eugene's interviews and play therapy, but had not yet met the boy in person. Sue brought him to the station. The detective kept it friendly but businesslike, even though on the inside he wanted to pick the kid up, give him a hug, and cry for him.

Forgan explained to Eugene that he was the lead investigator on the case.

"You're going to catch the bad man?" Eugene asked.

"I'm going to try."

But the Clark/Del Sordo investigation, as it was called in homicide branch, had to share manpower with other cases. In the early days after a murder, police flood the zone, but now, six months in, detectives had been dispersed to other assignments. Warren Korol was tied up with the Sukhwinder Dhillon double-poisoning trials, so detective Mike Thomas was brought on to replace him as case manager. And soon Thomas and Forgan would be assigned to help investigate the case of a woman's remains found in a field near African Lion Safari in Flamborough.

Forgan re-examined Charlisa's phone book and diary, and interviewed and re-interviewed people of interest. The most tantalizing piece of evidence so far sat in an OPP lab — the baseball bat. He learned from a biologist at the Centre of Forensic Sciences in Toronto that two DNA profiles had been developed from blood found on the bat: they matched Charlisa and Pat's DNA. But the palm impression on the bat handle still had no match. At the OPP lab, investigator Dave Sibley had compared that palm print with those belonging to more than a dozen people sent his way by Hamilton police. No luck.

Forgan made a pitch to his superiors in Hamilton: why not assign a willing ident guy to manually comb through the palm-print cards on file with Hamilton Police looking for a match? He was denied. They were short-staffed, the task would require unknown hours to wade through thousands of cards, and the suspect's print might not even be there.

In June 2001, the first anniversary of the murders, Forgan placed flowers on Charlisa's and Pat's graves. The cards read, "We promise to see that justice is served."

Sue tried to stay patient, kept telling herself that the investigation would take time. She spoke with Pat's mom, Ruth, who was bitter at how long the investigation was taking, and how it was being conducted. Ruth would often phone Forgan with suggestions and questions.

"Ruth," Sue told her, "they can't tell you anything."

Sue believed in Forgan, felt he was doing all he could. She found herself compulsively watching crime shows — *Law & Order, CSI* — as though vicariously searching for the killer through the television screen. And she wrote poetry, something she hadn't done since she was a little girl:

> I am drowning in the pain.
> It feels like you're living and sometimes you are, but I am
> drowning in the reality, and it is massive.
> The realization that you are never to be again, and never
> coming back, it is more than I can bear.
> I flip my mind to somewhere else to push the reality
> away, but there's no worse place in the whole universe.
> You are not coming back and the reality is drowning.
> A test of my faith, can I truly accept you in another form?
> Can I breathe your energy, can I stop drowning?

8

ROCK BOTTOM

Summer 2001
Cambridge, Ontario

Shane Mosher felt the barrel of the handgun grind into the back of his neck, forcing his head over the edge of the garbage dumpster. Urine ran down his leg. He heard himself pleading for his life, begging the man not to blow apart his skull.

That night Shane had done as instructed, entered the Chinese food restaurant, and left the paper bag on the counter. That was the signal. Leave the bag, place your order, and leave. He asked for an eight ball, which meant 3.5 milligrams of crack cocaine. He had just returned to make the pickup when a large man grabbed him from behind, pushed him out back behind the restaurant, to the dumpster, gun drawn.

"Are you a narc?" the man snarled.

"What, are you crazy?" said Shane, terrified. "What are you doing? Look, please, I've got a little girl. I'm nobody. I'm not a narc. I'll smoke the whole thing right in front of you!"

The man let him live. But Shane's old life was already dead. He was hooked on crack, and even after that night he kept using. He had started using in June, which was a year since his mom died. Shane was looking to numb his feelings and a guy he knew in Cambridge, a city just east of his home in Brantford, offered him a fix. Shane had never tried crack before.

"You'll love it," the guy said.

Shane inhaled the hit through a doctored-up asthma puffer, and the feeling — it seemed to him that was the answer, right there, for everything. The deeper into it he got ... it was weird, Shane felt like he was on the outside, studying the guys he used with, as though he himself were the only sane one. The others ... those guys were nuts! And yet he was doing it, too. He heard the other guys talk about how they lost it all through crack — their jobs, houses, families — but he kept using, too.

Through the summer and into August, Shane developed a routine. He slipped out of bed at 4:00 a.m. in his home in Brantford, while his wife and little girl slept. Out the sliding back patio door, in the car, 25-minute drive to Cambridge, get his crack fix. And each night Shane drove back home, high on crack, in disbelief, breaking it down, talking aloud to himself: "What is happening to me? I am nowhere near this person."

He was blowing his life with crack, knew it, and couldn't stop. Driving his family car back to Brantford in the middle of the night, the burgundy Altima, trying to beat it home before first light, he looked for signs. What was he supposed to do? Twice he thought he saw a shooting star, as though God were sending a message.

"Why is this happening!" he shouted in his car. "Is this how it's going to end?"

Back home he eased back into bed beside Shannon. She was a heavy sleeper; he never woke her up, but she knew something was going on with him that summer. She didn't want to ask questions, though; was busy with her job, raising Riley.

After an hour of restless sleep, Shane always got up for his job at a greenhouse. He had to keep reporting on time — the place was owned by Shannon's parents. It was a sauna in there; he sweated like crazy, dropped weight, even as he had already lost 30 pounds on his thin frame from the crack.

He looked like the addict he was, fading into oblivion, heading for the rock bottom he had seen other guys hit. He blew about $15,000 in three months on crack. Sunday night, August 12, for the first time he didn't make it home in time. Shannon called the hospital, worried. At 6:30 a.m. he pulled into the driveway. Shannon was standing on the front step, looking exhausted. Shane felt a sinking feeling inside, knowing this was it.

"You need to get help," she said, "or else you are out of here."

9

DEATH SENTENCE

One week later, on Sunday night, August 19, a woman wearing a red tank top, jeans, and running shoes entered a low-end bar called Big Lisa's. Located on King Street East in Hamilton, it was a dive where the clientele rarely used their own names. It had been raided earlier that summer by 30 police officers, and more than a dozen regulars were charged with drug-related offences and hauled to Central Station jail. Big Lisa's was shut down, but not for long.

The woman's name was Jackie McLean. At first she sat alone. Just after 10:00 p.m., she was joined by a couple of men. One of them had a tightly cropped haircut and teardrop tattoos under one eye. The guy seemed perpetually on edge, not quite all there. His name was Barry. Another guy joined them at the table. He had short red hair, a white, ribbed T-shirt. He introduced himself. His name, he said, was Carl.

Later that night Jackie ended up with the two men down the street, in a crevice of the city frequented only by those in the downtown crack cocaine subculture. It was one of the apartment units on the second floor of 193 King East, located above the Sandbar, a boarded-up tavern and former drug haven. There were just 11 active units in the building, and some of these were like clubhouses for addicts. The apartments where the addicts hung out reeked of a sweet pungent odour, like burnt plastic, from the crack; it mixed with the smell of urine and sex. Bare light bulbs hung from ceilings, clothes were strewn on floors, and the walls were marked with graffiti and dried rivulets of blood, the detritus of violence and needle use.

One floor up from where the group gathered to smoke crack was unit 4, often used for smoking up and sex transactions. Tonight it was unoccupied. Long ago unit 4 might have been a trendy place to live downtown, with the high ceiling and loft at the top of a steep staircase. From the loft, out the window, the Royal Connaught Hotel was visible in the distance. A broken down hotel now, it had once played host to royalty, prime ministers and movie stars.

Jackie entered the apartment with the man with red hair and the pale blue-grey eyes, the one named Carl. The lock didn't work; a fridge on the inside of the door was used to block it for privacy. Jackie helped slide the fridge across once they entered.

She had planned to leave town on a bus the next day, for a rehab centre in Niagara Falls. She would show everyone, especially her kids, that at 36 she was getting clean for good. She had no lack of motivation. A week earlier, August 12, her oldest child, Ashley, gave birth to her first grandchild. At Big Lisa's it was all Jackie had wanted to talk about.

Jackie was born November 17, 1964. Her mother was a woman named Christina Isabelle Howard, who everyone called Bella, and who had served in the military. Jackie's father was abusive to Bella, and so when Jackie was older, she decided to take the last name of her stepfather: McLean. When she was 18, Jackie had Ashley, her first of five children, and they lived with Bella, a strong woman who held the family together.

Jackie and her kids — Ashley, Brad, Candice, Danielle, and Patrick — moved around a lot in the city. For a time, living in the north end, Jackie had them take food to the homeless nearby, even as the family didn't have much to live on themselves. She had a raw sense of humour, and big dreams, but was a restless spirit, easily bored, and could not hold down a steady job. She also had a rebellious streak; she liked to party, but got in with the wrong crowd. It led to a crack cocaine addiction.

In 1994 Bella died from lung cancer. At her request, she was buried in her military uniform with her medals on. Jackie took it very hard, and soon after left her family for a few years, took a bus out west, to Calgary and B.C. Out west Jackie planned to take courses in secretarial work, turn her life around. Her kids stayed with family in Hamilton, including

Hamilton Spectator.

Jackie McLean.

Jackie's older sister, Cindy. Jackie would phone home, tell the kids she was clean, and was going to come home and be the mother she had always wanted to be, get everyone under one roof.

She returned to Hamilton in 2000, but was denied access to custody of her kids, given her lack of employment and her history of drug abuse. For a time she lived across the street from Ashley, near King and Wentworth. Her daughter would go to her place before school for breakfast. Jackie was determined to be a good mother, and Ashley yearned for it to happen. She knew what her mom was really like; that she was a caring, funny woman, but one who led a double life.

Back in Hamilton for just a few months, it was too easy for Jackie to run into the old crowd and renewed temptation. One night Ashley had a boyfriend over at her mom's place. To give them some space, Jackie said she'd go across the street to the bar for a drink — just one, she promised. But Jackie met a guy, they smoked up, and she was hooked again, bingeing. She started blowing her money on crack, and turned to prostitution to bankroll the addiction. Ashley worried about her constantly; she believed that crack addiction was often a death sentence.

In August Ashley awaited the birth of her child. She was 18, the same age her mom had been when Ashley had been born. Jackie told her she wanted to be there in the delivery room.

"Mom, if you aren't clean, you're not coming for the birth."

"Of course I will be; I'll prove it to you. I'm going to be the grandma."

Ashley had her doubts, but did not voice them. She always let her mom feel that she believed in her. And on the day of the birth, Jackie made it; rode a bus across town to McMaster, a bag of presents on her lap. She was ecstatic in the delivery room and was the first to hold the baby boy, Nathan, even as nurses tried to pry him loose to clean him up.

On August 16 Ashley talked to her on the phone. "How's my baby doing?" Jackie said.

"I'm fine, Mom."

"Not you, my other baby!"

Ashley wanted her mom to see Nathan one last time before Jackie went away to rehab in Niagara Falls. That afternoon she dropped by unannounced at an apartment downtown where Jackie was living. But she was gone.

"You just missed her," a friend said.

Ashley rushed out of the apartment, drove around the block, but could not see her mom anywhere.

And then came August 19, when Jackie entered Big Lisa's, as though needing to take one last dip in the wrong pool before getting clean. That night Jackie McLean was unable to stop it, unable to get off the train that hurtled toward her dark fate in unit 4 of the Sandbar. When it was all over, she lay on the floor of the loft, under a dust-caked fan high up on the cathedral ceiling. Out the window were chimneys, cloaked by the night, and further west, the Royal Connaught, a weathered monument to an era of glamour and chivalry, its neon red sign the backdrop for the final beat of Jackie's heart.

10

UNDERWORLD

Detective Dave Place awoke to the sound of his pager beeping on the night table. It was Monday, August 20. He looked at the clock: 4:18 a.m. Place grimaced. He tiptoed out of the bedroom, careful not to wake his wife, Joanne, or his young kids, and phoned Central Station. An inspector told him there had been a homicide: female in an apartment above the Sandbar Tavern on King Street East. Sexually assaulted, possible strangulation.

He showered, shaved, and put on a suit. Place — a muscular six foot five, 220 pounds — looked like he could break a man in two, yet he came across as soft-spoken, cerebral, his expression deferential. He had been in homicide for a year; his first case had been that of a man who stabbed his gay lover 18 times, once through the middle of a flaming heart tattoo.

Place arrived at the station to learn that he would be the lead investigator. He spoke with uniformed officers who had been at the scene, and made notes detailing witnesses he needed to check out. An officer handed him three bags of shoes taken from people who had been in the apartment that night.

Place reviewed information on a suspect in custody named Barry Lane. Barry was 29, had a long criminal record, outstanding charges against him in Newfoundland, and a caution in his file that he could be violent. Barry had been inside unit 4 above the Sandbar, where the body was found. His shoes had left bloody footprints on the floor.

At 7:00 a.m. Place went downstairs to the holding cells. Barry was there, looking gaunt. He had teardrop tattoos under one eye and reeked from smoking crack much of the night. He was both angry and paranoid.

"Hey, Barry, how are you doing?" Place asked.

"All right."

"Can I get you a coffee or something?"

"No."

"What I'm interested in is what's happened over at the Sandbar, and what you saw."

"This is bull!" Barry said, shouting. "I've been here four hours, locked up. They took my sneakers. I paid a hundred and fifty bucks for those sneakers yesterday. And they're gone."

"They're not gone. We have them."

"I want my sneakers back, man. This is, like, weird, man."

"Well, you have to understand, we're dealing with a murder, right?"

"I guess so."

When confronting a suspect, Place never tried to intimidate. His method was to just talk, build rapport, let the truth be revealed. He didn't even call it an interrogation; called it, rather, an interview. He treated it like a science; studied non-verbal clues, variances in language that tipped off when a suspect was lying.

"Listen, Barry, I'm not here to make your life miserable," Place said. "I'm a reasonable guy. Okay?"

"I want to go home, man."

"I've got a murder, a dead woman. My understanding is that you went into the scene with another man."

"I haven't f---ing done nothing, man. I just — buddy comes down the stairs, I was in buddy's apartment, smoking rock. The old guy comes downstairs, says the girl up there is dead. I said you're full of s--t. So I go upstairs. I saw the girl and I ran down the street. And the first thing I seen was a cop. I flagged a cop in. And I get locked up for five hours for this? 'Cause I flagged the cop in? And he takes my sneakers? That don't make no sense to me."

"No, it doesn't make sense."

Barry described the victim. Said there was blood on the floor at the top of the stairs where she lay, and that it looked like she had been raped.

"I swear on my daughter and my son's life that I never touched her."

"Okay."

"Never did! I just — I was at the wrong place at the wrong time."

Hamilton Police Service.

The inside of the old Sandbar Tavern, which was used as a crack house.

Barry was a suspect, but then he had also been the one to notify police on the street. Does the killer do that? And, Place could tell that Barry was offering strong denials, not evasive ones. Forensics could be critical, though; if his DNA was found on the victim, if it showed that he had had sex with her, that would be strong evidence against him. However, Barry readily consented to give a DNA sample.

At 11:00 a.m. Place visited the morgue at Hamilton General Hospital along with detective Mike Thomas, who had been assigned as case manager for the Sandbar murder, in addition to his work overseeing Clark/Del Sordo. The detectives left the hospital with forensic pathologist Dr. Chitra Rao and headed to the crime scene in unit 4.

It was as brutal a crime scene as Place or Thomas had ever witnessed. The picture of what had likely happened was all too clear: a pool of blood was evident on the first floor of the unit, and transfer stains on each of the 16 carpeted stairs up to the loft floor. The killer had dragged her up the stairs after the initial assault. At the top, on the loft floor, lay the victim, and more blood. She had been beaten, and from the torn clothes and body position, it was clear that she had been sexually assaulted. A steel bar with blood on it leaned against the wall.

The detectives spoke with the ident men, Bill Cook and Stan Marek, who had been working the scene, circling blood spatter marks on the walls, measuring spatter. It was a difficult scene to process, with blood from the homicide but also dried blood from other past incidents all over the walls.

Twenty minutes later Place left. He walked down the street to a construction site at the northeast corner of Walnut and King. He noticed loose bars of structural steel. He spoke to the site supervisor. "Last Friday I saw two pieces of steel tubing about 18 to 20 inches long on the west side of the building," the man told him. "There is only one there now."

Later, Place received a call from another detective called in to assist — Don Forgan, who, while still the lead on Clark/Del Sordo, had his hand in several other cases now. Forgan passed along an update, that the deceased had been officially identified through fingerprints from a criminal record. Her name was Jacqueline Heather McLean. Forgan added that the cause of death was severe injury due to multiple blows to the head.

The challenge for Place was compiling accurate information from witnesses who had seen Jackie that night, but who had also been smoking crack. Rumours spread through the drug underworld that the victim had been strangled and her body disemboweled. None of that was true.

During the course of more interviews, Place learned that Jackie had talked with a few men at Big Lisa's in the hours prior to her murder, and that a couple of these men had argued with her, accused her of shortchanging them on crack she had sold. This, he learned, was not entirely new: Jackie paid for crack on occasion through prostitution, and had ripped off clients. Barry was still on his radar as a suspect, but he was not looking strong, given his post-offence conduct. Place learned of another man, named Ken, who had been arguing with Jackie at the bar. He needed to find him. And there had been at least one other man who spoke with Jackie at Big Lisa's, and who had likely been with her above the Sandbar. Place was missing a key piece of the puzzle. He decided to re-interview some witnesses.

11

EVIL PRESENCE

On Monday morning, August 20, Shane Mosher entered a substance and withdrawal management treatment centre in Simcoe, a town one hour south of Hamilton. Shane's wife, Shannon, had driven him there from their home in Brantford for the first time a week earlier. She loved Shane and felt he was worth saving, along with their marriage. Shane was determined to kick his crack addiction, and never again put life with Shannon, and their little girl, Riley, in jeopardy. And now he was checking in for a second week of treatment. Shane had attended discussion groups, was doing well in rehab, and enjoyed the staff, the chats. He connected easily with people; he just had that way about him.

In a group discussion on Monday, August 20, Shane met someone who had checked in very early that morning. Young guy, red hair; he wasn't saying much in the group; kept to himself. He said his name was Carl. At first Carl didn't talk to anybody, and when he did talk, it nearly led to a couple of fights. But as the week wore on, he did talk to Shane. They seemed to have things in common. Both had grown up in the Maritimes. They talked sports. Carl wasn't much into athletics growing up, but he did box as a kid. Carl told Shane that the gym out east where he had trained always smelled of sweat mixed with the orange slices consumed by the boxers. To this day whenever he smelled oranges it took him back to that gym, he said. During breaks Shane and Carl threw a baseball around outside.

"Carl," Shane said, "why don't you get the bat from the shed, tap a few grounders out there?"

But Carl would not go to the shed, would barely look at it. Seemed odd. Shane had started observing Carl. It was something he did; he liked to take people's measure, figure out what made them tick. He could tell Carl was a hard guy, had rage inside, and seemed like the type who could snap at any moment. But still Shane chatted with him. Maybe he could help the guy.

They had rooms on the same floor of the house, and Shane noticed that Carl kept socks wedged in the spring-loaded door of the bedroom, all night, as though he was afraid to let it close. They continued to hang out together, and by Thursday Carl had started confiding in Shane, talked about hating his father, and told Shane his full name: Carl Hall. He said he was on the run after having robbed a bank in Hamilton.

That night, after the 11:00 p.m. curfew, it was silent in the house, and Shane heard a knock on his door. It was Carl. Shane invited him in. Carl wore green cargo pants and a T-shirt. He entered, shut the door, and sat on the end of Shane's bed. He held a pillow in his hands, and as he spoke, Shane watched him squeeze it tighter. He had a sense that Carl was about to tell him something very dark.

"Shane, I'm not on the run for robbing banks."

Carl Hall sat on the end of Shane Mosher's bed, rocking back and forth, white-knuckling the pillow clutched in his hands.

"I did something horrible," he said.

Carl told Shane a story. He had a girlfriend in Hamilton, he said, and they had a daughter. And Carl knew a guy; he did some drug deals with him. But then this guy harassed Carl's girlfriend, and his young daughter was there when it happened. There had to be payback. Shane, who lay on the bed, felt a shiver; goosebumps popped on his arms.

Carl continued. He told Shane that he went to this guy's apartment and noticed a white van outside the building. He walked up the stairs, had a baseball bat. A fridge blocked the door from the inside, but he was able to get it open. Inside, he saw this guy on his knees, beside a table. Carl hit him in the head with the bat. And again. He heard gurgling sounds. Carl knew it was serious. And then another person came in the room. A woman. Carl's voice grew sharper telling the story, almost angry.

"She wasn't supposed to be there, Shane," he said, his body shaking. "I knew what I had to do."

Ron Albertson, Hamilton Spectator.

Shane Mosher outside the rehab centre where he met Carl Hall.

Carl asked Shane not to tell his story to anyone. And he said that he was scared. Not of the police, but that karma would get him. That's why he kept his door propped open at night in the Holmes House rehab centre, he said: because he was scared of what might happen to him behind closed doors.

Shane kept his expression calm, but inside he was terrified. A killer, a double murderer — and maybe he had killed more than two people, he thought — was sitting on his bed, and had confided in him. What was he supposed to do? Carl left his room and walked back down the hall. Shane did not sleep all night. He made a decision.

The next morning, Friday, August 24, he packed his suitcase, waited for Shannon to pick him up to go home for the weekend. He was scheduled to resume rehab at the centre on Monday. Shane stood at the front door. Carl walked up to him, looked at the suitcase.

"Are you coming back?" he asked.

"Sure, Carl. I'll see you Sunday night," Shane said, trying to keep his voice friendly. Then Shane looked down at his own suitcase and saw it, right there on the tag: SHANE MOSHER. Along with his name, there was also his phone number, his family address in Brantford. Right there for Carl to see.

Shannon's car pulled up and Shane moved outside with his bag. She walked up the sidewalk to greet him, along with Riley. They were bathed in sunshine, yet there was a chill in the air.

Shane could feel himself shivering with fear, blood draining from his face. He looked back over his shoulder. There was Carl, on the veranda, looking down at his wife and child, this evil presence having now entered his family's life. And Shane had let it in. He was very quiet in the car as Shannon drove back to Brantford. Shannon, who had been heartened by her husband's progress in rehab for his crack addiction, knew something was up. Shane looked like he hadn't slept, was very pale.

Finally, he spoke. "I'm not going back," he said.

12

HATE MACHINE

Detective Don Forgan had no fresh leads in the double homicide and it was getting to him. The killer had been living free for 16 months. While the case remained ongoing, it was no longer on the front burner for the Major Crime Unit. He was ordered to move the Clark/Del Sordo file boxes out of the homicide office project room and into a storage area. Forgan met with Charlisa's father, Al Clark, who had been shattered by his daughter's death. It was a courtesy call, Forgan had no news to pass along. He continued receiving calls from the mothers, Ruth Del Sordo and Sue Ross, both seeking updates and offering suggestions for the investigation. Were police looking in the right places, they asked? Had they looked hard enough at Charlisa's ex as the suspect?

Forgan had planned to arrange a new polygraph for the ex, and he was still pushing for Pat's father, Flavio, to take the test as well. He even wondered about having Eugene sit with a hypnotist to see what other details he could remember from the night of the murders. There seemed no other avenues to pursue. He was getting tapped by his senior officers to work other cases, including revisiting the Sheryl Sheppard cold case, the first of his career in homicide, which still remained cold.

At that same time, Detective Dave Place was revisiting key witnesses in the Jackie McLean investigation. On October 25 Place interviewed a woman who had worked as a waitress at Big Lisa's bar on King East. Two months had passed since the murder, but she had good recall on details from Jackie's last night alive. She remembered Barry Lane, the guy with the teardrop tattoos, who had sat with Jackie in the bar. And, she said, there was another. He was about 25 years old, around five foot nine, strawberry red hair, trimmed goatee, lots of freckles. He wore a white, ribbed shirt and a grey coat. He had introduced himself as Carl. So far in the investigation Place had heard no mention of anyone named Carl. She said that Carl sat with Jackie at the bar, asked if he could buy her a beer, but she had said no. Later, she had seen Jackie with both Carl and Barry. It looked like the men were trying to convince her to get them some crack.

Back at the station, Place logged on to the Hamilton police mug shot retrieval system. He typed in the name Carl and the physical description. Up popped a name: Carl Ernest Hall. His last known address in Hamilton had been on Ferguson Avenue North. He was 27, sometimes known by the nickname "Reds." He had several prior convictions, and an outstanding charge for an assault in 2000 in Hamilton against a girlfriend named Crystal.

Lately, Carl had been causing trouble in Brantford, as well. On September 12 he was convicted in that city for uttering threats against a police officer and obstructing police. Place contacted the jail in Brantford. Carl was still incarcerated, but only for a couple more weeks on the Brantford charge. He had had one visitor: a woman named Lise, who wrote "friend" on the register.

Place later learned that Carl was filing a guilty plea on the Hamilton assault charge. He knew the plea offered an opportunity, and called the assistant Crown attorney prosecuting the case. Place wanted the Crown to push hard to have the judge order Carl to give a DNA sample as part of the sentence. The judge granted the request.

The importance of getting Carl's DNA increased when Place received a call from the Centre of Forensic Sciences in Toronto about a disturbing, and critical, piece of evidence that had been developed from the crime scene. A semen sample taken from Jackie McLean was determined to have been confined to the "high vaginal area." The substance had not migrated. Place knew what that had to mean. Whoever had intercourse with her had done so on the loft floor of the apartment above the Sandbar, after she had been dragged up the stairs — when she had been either dead, or nearly so. Place believed that the one who deposited that semen had to be the killer.

On October 30 the waitress from Big Lisa's came to the station to view a photo lineup — a series of portraits that included the suspect, and others. She pointed to the picture of Carl Ernest Hall as the man she saw in the bar with Jackie.

Meanwhile, Place worked to track down Carl's ex-girlfriend, Crystal. He learned that at one time Crystal had worked at a fast-food place downtown in Hamilton. Place reached her on the phone. She was wary of police, didn't want to get involved. He told her she was not in any trouble.

"This is a murder investigation," he said.

"Oh, no, not Carl, no way — this is the one above the Sandbar, right?"

"Yes."

Place wrote her words in his notebook. An interesting response. With little prompting she had specifically referenced a two-month old homicide, and was definitely not surprised they were looking for Carl.

On November 5 he interviewed Crystal. She told Place that she had dated Carl for a few years, and that when he was high on crack, he would stay awake sometimes for two or three days, wired, paranoid.

"God knows what that man is capable of," she said.

Their relationship had often been violent, she said. Carl had hit her, choked her; once he had stabbed her in the leg with a steak knife because she burned dinner. Crystal had responded to his attacks as well. She had punched him. Once she bit him on the leg, drawing blood. She said that Carl liked to rip her underwear before having sex. An interesting bit of detail, Place knew, given that the underwear of the victim had been ripped as well.

"The time frame that I'm most interested in," Place said, "is when you last saw Carl."

Crystal said that had been very early on August 20 — in the hours following Jackie's murder — when they met at the Wesley Centre downtown. She could smell crack on him, and a woman's perfume.

"I said to him, 'Well you're obviously rocked up. You're drunk and you smell.'"

She tried to break up with him. He begged her not to; said he loved her, he could change.

"He said that he did something bad, and I can't leave him now.

"I asked him, 'What did you do?'

Police surveillance video of Carl Hall with ex-girlfriend Crystal.

"He said he couldn't talk about it. He said he wanted to hitchhike out of the province. I said I wasn't going; I told him, 'You use your thumb and away you go.'"

After she repeatedly refused to leave with him, Carl punched her and spit in her face.

The interview with Place lasted an hour and a half. "Is there anything else that you can tell me, something I've forgotten to ask you or anything that's come to mind?" he asked.

"Whatever happens to him ... I will be there every court date to watch him go down," she said. "And I will testify against him. I hate Carl Hall with a passion. I hope that he rots in hell."

Carl was looking good as a suspect in the detective's book; he would look even better if his DNA matched semen from the crime scene — although Place knew that getting a sample processed through the National DNA Data Bank and then jumping through procedural hurdles to get a DNA warrant for a homicide investigation would take time.

Place had to tighten the case, eliminate other suspects. He knew that he couldn't be seen to have tunnel vision in the investigation. The murder was a circumstantial case; in court the defence could point to several men who had been with Jackie that night. One of those suspects was Barry Lane. Barry's footprint in blood had been found in the Sandbar apartment, but Barry had said he had only viewed the body. More importantly his DNA did not match the semen found on the victim. And then there was the man named Ken, who had also been seen arguing with Jackie that night. Place learned that Ken had died two weeks after the murder, of an Oxycodone overdose.

Carl had got into trouble in Brantford in the days following his release from rehab in Simcoe. He had met a girl in rehab; they had hooked up for a while — all good, he reflected — but then he went and shot off his mouth to the local cops in Brantford. Not very smart, he reflected later. Got 45 days dead time on that one.

After getting transferred from Brantford to Hamilton to be sentenced on the assault charge against Crystal, he was moved to a prison in Penetanguishene, an hour north of Barrie, to serve a five-month sentence. He figured: just do the time and get out. And as for other skeletons in his closet, Carl figured he was okay. The cops had shown no indication they had anything on him for the murders. In Penetang he told a couple of inmates that he was trying to lie low, avoid getting tagged for "a high-profile break and enter in Hamilton."

In jail he ripped off a thousand push-ups a day. At five foot eight, he bulked up to 225 pounds; bragged that his arms were 18 inches in diameter. He grew one fingernail very long and sharp, just in case he needed to eye-gouge. He imagined that he was building himself into a "hate machine."

On his ever-expanding chest, he had a tattoo of a shining cross, just like his dad had back east. His dad had always been tatted up. Young Carl once watched the old man carve an image of a snake on his own thigh using cork and a needle.

No one was tough enough to fight him one-on-one in prison. In the Penetang jail, he knocked a guy out in a fight, got disciplined for it. One time six guys jumped him, packing cups — Styrofoam cups, stuffed with wet toilet paper until they are hard and heavy — that had been stuffed into a sock, which was swung like a club. But it wasn't all bad. Carl got together with a couple of guys for parties. They drank homebrew: liquor made from crushed oranges, apples, bits of pineapple, and about 50 packets of sugar — all left to ferment in a garbage bag for a week. It was like pure alcohol. Carl got pretty wasted on it. Fruit schnapps with a kick, he called it.

A new name appeared on Don Forgan's radar in January, 2002: Carl Hall. The information had come through a circuitous route. An informant had passed the tip about Hall on to the RCMP. An RCMP officer out of their London, Ontario, branch had then contacted Warren Korol, Forgan's old partner in homicide. Korol demanded more: What was the name of the informant? He pressed the RCMP to reveal the identity so that they could interview the person. It could assist the investigation. But the RCMP was treating the source as a confidential informant and would not divulge the name.

Forgan had never heard the name Carl Hall in relation to the Clark/ Del Sordo case. The name was now forwarded to ident officer Hank Thorne. He had been sending palm prints from the crime scene to Dave Sibley at the OPP lab to check against the palm print found on the rubber grip of the murder weapon: the baseball bat. Now Thorne checked Hamilton's palm print manual card file, containing such things as all break-and-enters in the city, for Carl's name. He found a card on file for Hall, Carl Ernest. Thorne called Sibley and told him he was sending a new palm print for comparison.

Sibley had other work on the go, and after trying without success to match more than 25 palm prints already in the Clark-Del Sordo case over more than a year and a half, he was in no hurry to get to the latest.

On Thursday morning, February 25, Don Forgan arrived at Central Station to start his day shift. Guys were talking in the homicide office, joking around; it was loud that morning. His phone rang.

"Forgan, Major Crime Unit," he answered.

"It's Dave Sibley. I've identified your print."

"Just a minute, Dave," Forgan said.

Over the racket of detectives in the homicide office, he could barely hear Sibley tell him the news. He held the receiver to his shoulder. Forgan was not one to curse. This time was an exception.

"Shut up!" he yelled, but with added emphasis. And then: "Go ahead."

"It's Carl Hall."

"It's Carl Hall!" Forgan shouted.

Finally, 20 months after Charlisa and Pat's murders, Forgan knew who held the baseball bat that night. He had told Eugene he would catch the bad man. Looked like they had him — and that the mystery informant had been bang on.

Detective Mike Thomas walked over to Forgan. "Hall?" he said. "We're about to charge him on Jackie McLean."

13

PIPE DREAM

The detectives could see the walls closing in on the killer — for all three homicides. They knew that Carl was still in jail up in Penetanguishene, but time was not on their side. He would soon be a free man; on March 16 he was due to be released for the assault conviction he was serving. In fact Carl had been due to get out sooner than that, on March 9, but had been kept for another week due to bad behaviour. He had been fighting and had also pulled the fire sprinkler in his cell. Extending his sentence in prison was a costly mistake. Dominos were falling quickly.

On March 11 a judge granted Hamilton police a DNA warrant for Carl. The next day he was ordered in jail to provide a DNA sample. Four days later, on March 15, at 5:00 p.m., Detective Dave Place received a call from the Centre of Forensic Sciences in Toronto. It was a match: Carl Hall's DNA matched the high vaginal semen sample taken from Jackie McLean. That night, at 7:00 p.m., Place and Thomas checked out an unmarked white Crown Victoria and drove two hours to a Best Western hotel in Midland, 20 minutes from the jail in Penetang.

The next morning broke sunny and very cold. Just after 8:00 a.m., a guard called on Carl in his cell. He had visitors. Carl knew something was up after having been asked to give a DNA sample, but just what, he was not sure. He was led into an office where he saw two large men in suits. And now he knew what was happening. *They're gating me*, he thought — arresting him just as he was about to be released. Dave Place towered over Carl, diminishing him in the space.

"I am arresting you for the first-degree murder of Jackie McLean," he said. "You may also be charged with the murder of Charlisa Clark and Pasquale Del Sordo. Do you understand?"

"Yes."

Carl was cuffed with a waist chain and leg irons, and loaded into the Crown Vic. A Hamilton police cruiser followed behind. The detectives had a two-hour drive back to Hamilton. Dave Place got Carl talking.

"Any of your family know you're getting out today?" he asked.

"No, don't have any family," Carl said. "Black sheep. I have one sister; haven't talked to her in four years. My parents, four or five years."

"The girl that visited you in Brantford — is it Lise?" Place asked.

"Yeah."

"How do you know her?"

"She's from rehab."

"When were you in rehab?"

"In Simcoe, I'm not sure exactly the date. I figured you guys would know I was there."

"No, we missed that one. What's the name of that place?"

"Holmes House."

Carl told the detectives he had to use a bathroom. Mike Thomas pulled the car in at a sprawling highway service centre. The two detectives escorted him in, trying to conceal the cuffs. Thomas wondered what people would think if they knew they were in the presence of a triple murderer.

Back at Central Station in Hamilton, Place checked Carl into a cell just before 11:30 a.m. At 2:00 p.m. Place interviewed him. He asked about that night with Jackie McLean. Carl said they had sex in unit 4 above the Sandbar, but that he did not harm her; he said that they had both left the unit and returned downstairs to another where people had been smoking crack.

"Here's the problem we have," Place said. "She's killed in the apartment ... the one you're in with her. That's where she's found dead." Place told him about the high vaginal swab, indicating Carl's DNA on the victim.

"I hear what you're saying, but I can't explain it," Carl said. "I'm not going to change what I said; I can't explain it."

Place showed Carl a photo of the metal bar, the murder weapon.

"That's the weapon that was used to cave in her head."

"Okay."

"And there's no question as to the finding, that you're responsible for her death.... Did you kill Jackie?"

"No."

"What happened in there?"

"I told you."

"Yeah, but it wasn't the truth."

"As I know it to be."

Place moved on to ask him about the murders for which he had not yet been charged, of Charlisa and Pat.

"Can we just take a break a bit?" Carl replied. "This is all just nuts."

Place left for a moment. Alone in the room, Carl looked up at the video camera.

"This is crazy," he said to himself, then swore several times. "How did I get caught up in this?"

When Place returned, Carl said he didn't want to talk anymore, not without his lawyer.

"Is there any reason," Place continued, "that your fingerprints would be found in [Charlisa's] apartment?"

"I don't know. I know people that used to live there.... So we are done with the questions now. Okay?"

"Charlisa?" Place said. "Does that name sound familiar?"

"Not really."

"She goes by Char. And her boyfriend was Pat."

"No, I don't know them."

"Is there any reason your palm print would be on a bat in that apartment?"

"No, unless it was Paul's." Paul was a former tenant of that apartment, and a friend of Carl's.

"Would it surprise you to know the prints were there?"

"Yeah, a little bit. Maybe when I was there and sold pot ... I don't, I can't see it. You guys are way out in left field."

Carl asked if Place was charging him with the double murder.

"Should I?" Place asked.

"Go ahead."

"Did you kill them?"

"No. No, I don't even ... no. That's crazy. No. I never killed anybody."

"Should I believe you?"

"Yeah."

"Why should I?"

"Because I'm telling you straight."

Place told him that an informant had said Carl confessed to a double murder.

"If you say so, but that's unbelievable," Carl said.

"How would someone be in a position to pass that on to us?"

"I don't know…. I think it sounds like a pipe dream. You guys are way off base."

"How do you think everything's going to turn out, when all is said and done with?"

"I'm not worried…. You're barking up the wrong tree."

After two hours of questioning, Place left. Carl looked up at the camera again. "A pipe dream," he said, shaking his head, cursing.

Warren Korol, who had been watching the interview on a monitor in another room, entered. "I know you think this is a pipe dream, Carl," Korol said. "But you know, there is somebody out there, you admitted to them that you killed two people. I'm going to find that person."

"Okay, but that's inaccurate. I never did it."

"It's no pipe dream, Carl."

Carl had been pressured by Place, but now there was something about Korol's coolly aggressive manner that bothered him. Korol stared at Carl as though he knew what made him tick, like he was trying to bore a hole through his eyes and out the back of his skull. Carl did not like it.

"Carl," Korol said, "you need some help, bud."

"I need help," Carl said, sarcastically.

"You do. You need help."

Korol continued: "How did your palm print show up on the bat out of the blue? It was her baseball bat."

"If you're so sure about it, why don't you charge me?"

"One day I will charge you for that double murder. You'll be charged for three murders. You need some help, Carl."

"I'm not — I'm not sick."

"You need some help. You do. You've got some troubles, my friend."

14

THE RIGHT THING

With Carl locked away in Barton Street jail, Forgan, Thomas, and Korol met to review the details of Carl's confession that the informant had provided through the RCMP. Korol read the points aloud to the others: male and female victims; baseball bat weapon; white van outside the apartment; a fridge blocked the apartment door. Carl had to move it out of the way.

Mike Thomas, unique among the three detectives, knew crime scene details from both the McLean and Clark/Del Sordo murders. He spoke up. "Pardon me, what was that about the fridge?" he asked.

He knew that the fridge behind the door had been in the Sandbar apartment, not Charlisa's place. "It's the same guy; the killer is mixing details of both homicides into one story," Thomas said.

They had to find the informant, get his statement on the record, and get him to testify in court. Korol kept pressuring the RCMP: they needed the name. The RCMP officials refused; a confidential informant could not be named. Korol was bitter. It wasn't just about getting another witness in line. If the informant's identity remained a secret, the defence would surely point at the tipster as an alternative suspect once the case came to court. The defence would raise the issue of who had intimate knowledge of the double homicide. Was it Carl Hall? Or was it the guy who ratted him out? Maybe the guy assisted in the murders. Maybe he was the killer and was framing Carl. Korol knew that they couldn't risk that; he knew they had to find the informant.

"A guy like Hall has to confess to someone when he's at his lowest point," Korol said.

In his car-ride interview from Penetang, Carl had mentioned attending Holmes House for rehab. On March 28 Forgan, Thomas, and Korol checked out a car and headed to Simcoe. They had a search warrant for the rehab centre, to check records to see if Carl had been treated there. Maybe they could learn who he had confided in — a counsellor, perhaps. Before executing the warrant, they spoke informally with the manager to try and glean some information quickly. The detectives said they were investigating a homicide case involving a man named Carl Hall.

"Carl? I remember him being here," the manager said. "He admitted to a resident named Shane Mosher that he murdered two people."

The three cops stood there, stunned at first. There are those rare moments in homicide where you have a Hollywood "x marks the spot" moment, when time seems to stand still. The detectives looked at each other and smiled. The informant. Knew it. Finally, Forgan spoke. "Well, that's why we're here," he said cheerfully.

The knock on the door at a house in Brantford came later that day. A man answered. Slim, dark hair, boyish face.

Shane looked at the three men in suits, all of them clean cut; he could smell their cologne. "I bet you guys are from Hamilton," Shane said. "I figured you'd show up one day."

He agreed to come to the Brantford police station for an interview. He told Forgan he had passed along Carl's confession several months earlier, to an uncle of his named Don Scott, a retired RCMP officer. Shane had asked that his name be kept confidential; his uncle assured him it would.

Forgan asked him if he wished to have a lawyer present for the interview. Shane thought that he would like that at first, then changed his mind. He was now ready to jump in with both feet. And he had sensed from that moment in Holmes House, when he knew he would inform on Carl, that it would go like this. He wasn't crazy about the idea of having his name out there, but knew it was probably inevitable. Still, while relieved to hear that Carl was in custody, he was fearful, if Carl was released or found not guilty in court, that he'd be coming after Shane and his family. When the detectives told him that Carl had been taken into custody for a charge in Brantford, fear rippled through him. He wondered if Carl had ended up in Brantford looking for him, to exact payback.

Shane told Don Forgan everything Carl had confessed to him. As he spoke the goosebumps returned; Shane shook with the memory of that night. He was going to be an effective witness on the stand, Forgan reflected. The detectives dropped Shane off at his home. Warren Korol turned to Shane's wife, Shannon. "You should be proud of your husband," he said. "He did the right thing."

Forgan now tightened the screws on the case. He found a man living in Toronto named Paul, who had been a previous tenant at 781 King East, Charlisa's apartment. Carl's confession to Shane had suggested that Carl killed Pat and Charlisa out of mistaken identity — that he intended to get payback on a drug dealer. The man named Paul admitted he had indeed known Carl and sold him drugs. There had been a dispute between the two.

Was it enough to offer a motive? Perhaps it was, given that Carl was a man prone to anger and violence, and that he was routinely high on crack for days at a time. And Forgan now knew, through Shane, that Carl was feeling anger the weekend of the double murder for not being allowed to see his daughter on Father's Day.

On April 16, 2002, Carl Hall was charged with the murder of Charlisa Clark and Pat Del Sordo. Before the news was released to the media, Forgan informed the families. When he met with Charlisa's mother, Sue Ross, she wept, feeling pain and regret. The murders, she now knew, were a random act. Her Char had been in the wrong place at the wrong time. She couldn't help but reflect that if Sue had helped find Char a different apartment than the one on King East, her girl would be alive. Don't do that to yourself, others told Sue. She could not have known what would happen. Yes, yes, of course, Sue knew all that, the logic of it, but it was no good. She had failed to protect Char. The guilt would not fade; Sue could not stop retracing her steps, as though doing so might retroactively turn back time and alter Charlisa's fate. Why that apartment, of all the places in the city? For that matter, why did Sue even have to get remarried — if she hadn't, maybe she would have lived with Char, in a nice house, and she'd still be alive.

A week after the arrest, Forgan came by Sue's house for Eugene's fifth birthday party. The boy now knew that the bad man was in jail. He cheered when he heard the news. It was, Eugene thought, the best birthday present ever.

15

BITTER JUSTICE

At the preliminary hearing, family members of Jackie, Charlisa, and Pat heard details of the murders and watched video of the crime scenes. At one point Ruth Del Sordo experienced something very odd. She was certain, after a court officer turned on the crime-scene video from the apartment, showing her murdered son's body, that while the judge and lawyers could see the images on the screen, she could not. The picture appeared fuzzy; she could not make out anything. To her it was as though a higher power was protecting her from seeing Pasquale like that.

Charlisa's father, Al Clark, meanwhile, confined to his wheelchair, burned with rage seeing Carl Hall in the prisoner's box at the hearing. If he were able, he felt that he would jump over the barrier and take the guy out himself.

Jackie McLean's older sister, Cindy, was a regular in court. At times she cried, but other times she just felt so angry. She felt like she could kill Carl if she had the chance. She stared at him in court, trying to make eye contact, send a message. At one point he looked right back at her, his expression flat.

The video and photos at the prelim were difficult to watch, but what Cindy would always regret the most was having gone to the morgue to view her sister's body. Detectives always urge family not to view a loved one in the morgue after a homicide. Family members usually want to feel close to their loved one one final time, but it is never a good idea. It can leave mental scars that never heal. Still, Cindy had insisted. She could never forget how cold it had felt in that room, nor could she ever erase that image of her baby sister.

After the funeral Cindy had felt some comfort having made sure to provide Jackie with the proper resting place, one she would have wanted. It was right next to their mother, their beloved Bella. Cindy wrote a note to their mom, put it in plastic and buried it with Jackie: "I know you're waiting for her, so here she is, waiting for your lovely arms."

Ashley, Jackie's eldest child, also attended the preliminary hearing every day.

Her friends worried about her, worried that she'd be overwhelmed by the stress she was going through. It was true that Ashley had been upset during the investigation. After the police had vacated the Sandbar crime scene, she had sent her boyfriend to check it out for her, look for clues. Crazy, but she couldn't help it; she had to do something. And if anyone mentioned hearing a rumour about the case, she would corner them, ask them for more information. In court it seemed surreal to her, seeing the crime-scene photos. It was like the victim she was seeing was someone else, not her mother.

When Jackie was alive, she would give Ashley small gifts here and there. One of them was a Nike T-shirt that Jackie had herself worn. Ashley didn't think much of the gift at the time, but now she treasured it and wore it often. She never stopped seeing her mom in her dreams. In one of them, Jackie appeared and said to Ashley, "This is the last time you'll see me." And Ashley argued with her: "No, Mom, you're wrong. It's not." She kept having that same dream, over and over.

Ruth and Flavio Del Sordo purchased a plot in the City of Angels cemetery near their home, and a big stone monument as well, for the three of them: Pat, Ruth, and Flavio. They did not want Pat to lie alone; someday they would join him. After Pat's burial Ruth went to the cemetery two, three times a week. She was unable to stand at the stone, though. It was too emotional. Instead she knelt before it, speaking to her Pasqua, updating him on what was going on.

Ruth's sadness never waned and neither did her anger. She lamented aspects of the police investigation and the trial. Justice for Ruth was bitter. Even with the arrest of Carl Hall, she still felt that the system had failed her son, and still believed there had to have been more than one attacker. For the entire family, Pat's loss remained a wound that did not heal. None of the Del Sordos attended counselling. But Ruth wanted to talk about her son. All her kids were wonderful, but her first-born was a special light, and she would never be the same. When prompted she could barely bring herself to stop talking about her boy: how much he loved his family, life; what a breath of fresh air he was, such a ball of energy; how he was always there for her, a friend and confidant and son all in one. But she could not find many ears close to her to listen. For others in the family, even years after the murder, it remained too raw. It was not a subject to bring up.

When Pat's sister got married, Pat's father, Flavio, could not bring himself to enter the church to go and meet the priest in advance. He had not been a consistent churchgoer before his son's death, and after the murder he had lost his faith entirely. God had let him down. Ruth? She still had faith, but it prompted more questions than she could answer. If God willed all, if everything happened for a reason, why did this happen to her Pasquale? Words did not comfort, nothing did. She could never again play Pat's music; his CDs were packed away in the house. She could not play any kind of music without thinking of him, and so she avoided it entirely. Such a waste, she lamented, losing Pat's smile and joy; and also what he would have lovingly created with his talent for woodworking, a passion that ran in his blood.

But Ruth at least felt a smile when she remembered a line from the Book of John spoken by one of the readers at his funeral: "In my Father's house are many rooms. If it were not so, I would have told you. I go to prepare a place for you."

"Yes," one of Pat's brothers added in the church, "and now He will have many more rooms, and have the best carpenter to build them."

16

THE LOST BOY

The first of the two trials was scheduled to begin in the spring of 2005, but Carl fired his lawyers, delayed the process further. The Jackie McLean trial started, finally, in January 2006, before a jury and Superior Court Justice Jane Milanetti. Carl continued to cause trouble during the trial. He threatened courtroom guards, refused to enter court several times. Six Hamilton police officers were added for extra security.

"The position of the Crown," assistant Crown attorney John Nixon told the jury, "is that this murder was committed during the course of a sexual assault, and that, by definition, is first-degree murder."

The Crown argued that Carl had struck Jackie in the head six times with the steel pipe, and then had had sex with her when she was dead or dying. Carl's defence lawyer, Michael Puskas, called Barry Lane to the stand as an alternative suspect. But the forensic evidence that the Crown argued linked Carl to the sexual assault in the loft of the apartment proved critical for the jury. In the end, after a six-week trial, it took the jury just 10 hours to render its verdict: Guilty. First-degree murder. Carl was sentenced to life in prison with no eligibility of parole for 25 years. He stood in court after the verdict was announced.

"I have no remorse for something I didn't do," he said. "I thought justice should be done. So the woman is dead. Now, basically, I'm dead, too."

He was led from the prisoner's box. On his way out, he turned to a detective in the crowd. "Dave Place," Carl said, "you're a goof."

It was, reflected Place, a curious remark from someone as violent and foul-mouthed as Carl. In Carl's odd way, it might have been something of a show of respect. But then, Place did not spend time trying to psychoanalyze the man. Carl had done wrong and left evidence. Place followed it. It felt good to hear the conviction.

But as it happened, the case was not yet closed on the Jackie McLean homicide.

Just over a year later, on May 17, 2007, assistant Crown attorney Ed Slater rose for his opening remarks in the Clark/Del Sordo trial. Carl was defended by Russell Silverstein, a Toronto lawyer who had represented Hamilton serial poisoner Sukhwinder Dhillon in two high-profile homicide trials. Silverstein had lost both, but had mounted strong defences in each.

Slater began by telling the jury the story of Charlisa's son, Eugene, the "lost boy," who Constable Randy Carter had helped the day after Father's Day in 2000. He then described Carter's discovery of the crime scene. Slater spoke of the murders, the baseball bat, Shane Mosher's meeting with Carl Hall, and the confession. Don Forgan sat in court. The room was dead quiet yet electric with emotion. Forgan thought Slater's address was the most powerful opening he had ever heard. The detective studied the jurors, saw a couple of them wipe tears away. Evidence had not even been presented yet, but Slater had them already.

"The case that you are about to hear," Slater said, "has everything to do with what Randy Carter found when he took that boy home."

Carl listened in the prisoner's box. What was it that stirred inside him? Did the talk of the little lost boy, the one that Carl had seen the night of the murders, get to him? The boy was the one Carl had spoken of with regret, the one victim who gave him pause. Later, Carl would wonder about his motivation for what he did next. Was it a crisis of conscience? He didn't think that was it. In the past he had wondered if he had been born without one. No, he was more than ready to try to beat the rap. It was more a calculation of the odds.

His lawyer confirmed for him that the Crown would lead with evidence of his palm print on the bat. Not good. Maybe, Carl thought, he could run with the story that he had held the bat another time, prior to the murders, when visiting the former tenant, Paul. Or, he could say the cops had fabricated the evidence. Carl recalled having wiped it down after the murders. How could they get a print from it? But then, part of him just wanted to get it over with. He killed them and he wanted it to end.

That first day of the trial, after Slater's opening address, court took a recess. Behind closed doors Carl wept. That same day he decided to enter a guilty plea. There would be no trial. A week later he was sentenced to two counts of second-degree murder. He would serve three concurrent life sentences. And Charlisa's and Pat's families were spared going through a public trial, where the evidence from the crime scene would be shown in court for all to see.

The confession also meant that Shane Mosher would not have to take the stand, which was fine by him. Shane continued to live in the Hamilton area, and got a new, solid job. One of the detectives had called Shane a hero for his role in the investigation, and his wife, Shannon, was proud of him. Shane had taken the stand once in court, at the preliminary hearing into the double murder. He was frightened, having to walk past Carl to take the stand. It was the first time they had seen each other since the rehab centre. He testified in court to the confession Carl had made, and he felt Carl's eyes on him the whole time, but no words were spoken. Later, he worried that if he did not testify effectively, the whole case would blow up and Carl would be a free man to come after his family.

With Carl locked away, he and Shannon could breathe again, and he felt no urge to use drugs. He thought often of the road he had travelled. In the depths of his addiction, he had called out to God, wondered why it was happening. In retrospect he felt he knew. Only by going through that ordeal was he taken to Carl, and put in a position to hear the confession and contact police. In fact it seemed to Shane that his whole life had, in a sense, been a prelude to that horrible summer: growing up out east, which gave him a connection with Carl when they met; and all the curious twists in the road along the way. It was like it had all been meant to be from the start.

At sentencing, Carl came face to face one more time with the boy. Eugene had recently turned 10. He was offered the opportunity to present a victim-impact statement in court. He wanted to do it. Dressed in a suit and tie, the blond-haired boy rose from his seat and took the stand. With

Carl sitting close by in the prisoner's box, Eugene looked out at all the people in the courtroom, and began.

"Hello, your honour," he said.

Eugene thanked the Crown, and Don Forgan and Mike Thomas. The detectives sat together in court; the entire room pulsed with emotion; some in the audience quietly sobbed as the boy spoke. Forgan felt so proud of him, of how brave he was to be up there.

Eugene could see that his uncle, Charlisa's brother, Greg, was choked up. It was the first time he had ever seen Greg cry, and that made him feel emotional. But Eugene was determined to hold it in. He felt very mad at Carl Hall. But he was not going to let Carl Hall see him cry.

"Thank you for letting me talk today," he continued. "I have been waiting a long time for this day. On June 18th, 2000, I was three years old. I had a great room, lots of toys, a bike and a goldfish, and a mom that loved me a lot. When I woke up that morning everything changed. I saw lots of blood. I was scared and I will never forget. I know how life was, I know — shoot, now I live with my grandma and uncle. I still get scared when it is night time. And now I call my grandma my mom."

The boy in the suit stepped down from the stand, without a single tear in his dark eyes — Charlisa's eyes — and walked past the killer. And then, out of the courtroom, when it was all over, behind closed doors, Eugene cried, a lot.

EPILOGUE

A cold hard wind blowing off Lake Ontario meets the razor wire and guard towers of 175-year-old Kingston Penitentiary in eastern Ontario. The place has a medieval feel to it; visitors enter through a hulking front door into a lobby that is dark and cramped.

No friends or family come to visit Carl Hall. His uncle came and saw him back when he was in the bucket, in Barton jail in Hamilton. But not here. He is not in touch much with his family. He doesn't blame his upbringing for the way he turned out. He wrote his parents a letter soon after he was jailed for the murders. "It wasn't your fault," he said. He was the one who did it, period.

Talking to a writer, Carl now reconsiders the letter. "Is it my dad's fault? I guess that's up for debate. I can't say, 'Oh, poor me.' Won't use that as a scapegoat. On the East Coast, you grow up hard; that's just the way it is."

There is a trailer at the pen where inmates with good behaviour can enjoy conjugal visits. Carl misbehaves in jail, gets in fights. He tells inmates he's a nice guy, and if he's in the wrong, he'll apologize. But if he's right, and you cross him, he'll kill you. In any case no one comes to see Carl for a conjugal visit, either. He does look forward to just hanging in the trailer alone, though; looks forward to making himself some food, watching DVDs in peace.

He has never stopped denying murdering Jackie McLean. In prison Carl has continued to point the finger at Barry Lane, who also spent time with Jackie on the last night of her life. Carl says that the sex he had with Jackie was consensual, and that he left her that night "alive and kicking." The notion that he would have sex with a woman who was dead or nearly dead is crazy, he says. Certainly, that reputation would not help in prison. In the inmate culture, rapists and child molesters are not treated well. He blames police for falsely portraying him as a serial killer.

"Anyone can be a killer. Doesn't mean I'm a serial nutbar or something like that?" He tells the writer that he hopes he is "humanized" in a story being written about him. "I'm just a working dude, a normal guy who got into a bad scene.... The drugs made me a man that I'm not, brought out the worst in me."

As for murdering Charlisa and Pat, he never mentions them by name. He says not a day goes by he doesn't regret what happened. "I would give away my life for them if it would bring them back."

Why did he do it?

He claims that it was just a break and enter. He wasn't hitting the place to get revenge on anyone. Just broke in because he could see that the balcony door on King Street East to the apartment was open. He saw a guy sleeping on the bed, lights on in the room; he grabbed the guy's pants on the floor to get his wallet, and the guy grabbed his hand, fought back. So Carl hit him with the bat, again and again; and the woman, she was in the bed too, started screaming. So he killed her, too.

"The guy put his hand on me; I was terrified; I fought for my life. He was a lot bigger than me. And the rage ... I just kept going."

His story seems off. Pat's body was found face down on the mattress, as though he had never moved from a resting position. Charlisa's body, on her knees, suggested that she had been standing up, had come in from the hallway. It seems more likely that Carl killed Pat in cold blood, an attack from behind from which Pat had no chance to defend himself.

Carl does not sound angry at Shane Mosher for talking to police. He confessed to Shane to get it off his chest, and it felt good. He figured he had fudged enough of the details, but realized he had talked too much. Never thought Shane would tell. Regrets it now. Never should have told him.

He is not religious, but sometimes he says a prayer, asks God to forgive him his sins. Carl hints at other dark things he's done in his past, "a whole other incident" that has not been made public. He could say some things that could really screw him, he says.

As he approaches 40, the pale skin, red hair, and pudgy cast to his face and frequent smirk make him look younger. Physically, he is far from what he calls the "hate machine" he was building in jail prior to his convictions, when he worked out like a demon. The muscles have softened; he is overweight. All he does now is watch TV, read.

All of this is a woman's fault, Carl claims. He had a girlfriend, a long-distance relationship with a Hamilton girl named Shellee. For four years, while he was in jail awaiting trial, they dated, talked about getting married. On his fingers, Carl has the tattoo "SH" for Shellee Hall. But she broke up with him. Just as well, he figures; he wants to get back in a groove, get back in shape.

He reads mystery fiction, Stephen King, Grisham. He is a big fan of *Dexter*, the darkly twisted TV show about a vigilante forensic investigator who is a serial killer — but of bad guys. Does Dexter remind Carl of his experiences?

"Yeah, a bit. Although I never killed anyone who deserved it. That's the problem."

Early in 2012 his appeal of the Jackie McLean conviction was upheld by the Ontario Court of Appeal. The court ruled that the presiding judge in the first trial had made errors in her charge to the jury, for example, failing to "direct the jury's attention to some of the important evidence that was capable of supporting (the defence's) claim that Barry Lane was the killer." The original judge, the Court of Appeal ruling said, should have directed the jury to consider "his presence and strange behaviour soon after the deceased's body was found; … the fact he was not wearing a shirt after the murder; [and the fact that] his bloody footprints were found in the apartment leading away from a pool of the deceased's blood."

A new trial was ordered and began in the spring of 2012 in Hamilton. Carl would be tried before a judge only, no jury.

His lawyer was again Russell Silverstein, the same lawyer who had represented him in the Clark/Del Sordo trial.

Ron Albertson, Hamilton Spectator.

Life has been difficult for Sue Ross since Char's murder.

Members of Jackie's family followed the case in court. So too did Sue Ross, Charlisa's mother. During the trial Carl often stared at Sue, for long moments. He knew who she was, had seen her in court many times.

There was no expression on his face. He just stared. She had no idea what was going through his head. She just stared back at him.

The Crown argued that blood spatter evidence suggested Carl Hall had had sex with Jackie McLean after she had been bludgeoned with the steel pipe. Russell Silverstein offered a competing theory: the victim had had consensual sex with Carl, and then put her stained underwear back on, only to be murdered later on by the real killer — who the lawyer suggested was Barry Lane.

Silverstein also said that, given the pooling of blood on the apartment floor from the beating, if Carl had been the killer, one would expect there to have been blood on his shoes or other clothing — but there was none. The only person who had blood on his shoes was Lane.

In Canadian criminal law, the standard for convicting an accused of first-degree murder is that the court must be convinced of guilt "beyond a reasonable doubt." On June 23, 2012, after a two-week case, Ontario Superior Court Justice J.R. Henderson announced he was acquitting Carl Hall of Jackie's murder. He said the weakness with the Crown's case was that Carl's fingerprints were not found on the murder weapon, and no blood was found on his clothing.

The *Hamilton Spectator* reported that the moment the judge announced his verdict one of Jackie's daughters ran from the courtroom. And as Carl was about to be led away by police officers, Cindy McLean, Jackie's older sister, called him an asshole. Carl, in turn, looked over his shoulder and smirked at the family.

There was a police officer in the courtroom who watched it all unfold with a sense of disbelief. As the evidence had been presented for a second time, Detective Dave Place at first felt confident. He had a cautious nature when it came to trials, but in this case he couldn't help it. The semen and blood spatter evidence seemed to him overwhelming; clearly, the jury in the first trial had felt that way.

He had watched Russell Silverstein raise issues with the Crown's evidence, and to Place, the case for Carl Hall seemed weak at best. The lack of blood spatter on Carl's clothing, he felt, was a non-issue. Carl had said in a police interview that he had removed his pants prior to having sex with Jackie — so obviously his pants would have no blood spatter on them.

But toward the end of the trial, when Place heard that Silverstein had submitted a 57-page submission to the judge detailing closing arguments, he started to wonder if Carl had a shot at getting off.

As the judge presented his acquittal decision, Dave Place felt numb. He knew they had gathered strong evidence. His heart ached for Jackie's family. He understood and respected the Canadian judicial process. But he left the courtroom that day still firm in his belief that Carl Hall had gotten away with Jackie McLean's murder.

Russell Silverstein said the acquittal gave his client "a fighting chance" at being released from prison one day.

But even with his name cleared of the McLean homicide, the shadow of his admitted double murder in the Clark/Del Sordo case would always remain, and Carl was well aware of what that meant.

"I'm never getting out," he said in prison. "Maybe when I'm 70. But I won't live that long.... I just don't care."

If Canada had the death penalty, would he deserve it?

"I guess I do deserve it. And I'm growing less scared of dying, because life doesn't have much to offer."

"More coffee?" The elderly customer nods yes at her question but does not smile. The server, in her red uniform, hair up, tops up his mug, steam wafting, and returns to the kitchen. The woman waiting tables used to teach ballet. But now she works in the Zellers restaurant, in Hamilton's hard-bitten east end, where today the smoke from industrial stacks is frozen against a leaden sky. In the kitchen she chats with other, much younger servers. They are good girls. She has told them about her daughter, Charlisa.

The girls adore Sue Ross, her openness, her sense of humour. She is a brave and resilient woman, but they can always tell when she's feeling down. She is like a mom to them. Sue likes that. The girls remind her of Char. But at the same time it also makes her wary. She does not want to get too close. That's one reason she hesitated returning to teaching ballet; she was not ready to open her heart again. She does have her moments, though. Her co-workers at Zellers convinced her to get together for a backyard summer party. They had more than a few drinks, a lot of smiles — it was nice.

Hamilton police officer Randy Carter reunites with Eugene ten years after he had helped the lost toddler.

After the trial, Sue continued living in the tiny old house in the east end with her son. Greg, who is in his mid-twenties, and little Eugene. Sue's first husband, Charlisa's father, Al Clark, died a couple of years ago. Sue and her second husband, Bruce, split up not long after the murder. She had obsessively watched crime shows on TV in the time leading up to the trial, but when it was over, she could no longer watch any of it, turning instead to lighter fare, comedies. She does not look for silver linings, but at least she did ultimately find out that her belief that Char had been pregnant at the time of her murder proved not to be true. The autopsy showed that had not been the case. Pictures of Char continue to adorn her home, as do cows — Char collected cow-themed ornaments, mugs, and so friends of Sue keep giving them to her as gifts.

As for Eugene, he no longer has a biological mother, and has no desire to get to know his biological father. Greg, Charlisa's brother, is his uncle, but he is more like a big brother. Greg did his best after losing Char to help make Eugene's upbringing as positive as he could, give him some solid, traditional memories that he could reflect back upon when he got older; of Christmases and birthdays and trips.

Greg often thinks about his sister. He will never forget the time he babysat for Char at her apartment a few weeks before she died. When she got home from her night out, she gave him a big hug. She hadn't done that in a long time. He's careful not to let himself linger too long in sorrow. Char would not want that. But memories like that still get to him.

Greg is a burly-looking guy, big arms, looks like he should be playing football. But he is also soft-spoken; inside he is a lot like Charlisa: artistic in his way, a thinker, a seeker. He studied to be a chef, yearning to travel, discover the world. He chose instead to stay and help his mom raise Eugene. His life is on hold in a sense, has been since Charlisa's death. The killer did that to him. So for now, short of actually slipping the bonds of his hometown, he reads Jack Kerouac's *On the Road*, and imagines.

As for Eugene, as he neared his 13th birthday, he seemed like a regular kid. He told only his closest friends about his story. "Sometimes someone will ask me, 'How's your mom?' And I say, 'I have to tell you something; I call my grandma mom, because my mom passed away, she got murdered when I was three.' I tell them I was there."

There are times he thinks about what happened that night, and what he might have seen, but not very often. Sometimes he sees it in his dreams. It does not upset him to talk about it. Perhaps he was young enough that, while the memory exists, it is not strong enough to define him. The distant past is an old skin he has been able to mostly shed — a part of him, but separate at the same time. The fact that he was so young at the time of his mother's murder is tragic but maybe it also saved him.

At bedtime Eugene does not pray, but he talks to his mom, asks her how she's doing, what she is up to. He figures she's having fun somewhere with her grandfather, and Brody, their old dog, who died a while back. Eugene enjoys his video games; there's one he plays called *Resident Evil*. He is a strong player, working the controls, staring at the screen. His secret, he says, is that he does not blink.

He's not sure what he wants to be when he grows up. He thought for a while about being a cop. One day Don Forgan took him to the Hamilton Police Association's private club. Forgan sprung for wings and beer — root beer for the boy. Eugene likes Forgan a lot. That night the boy inhaled a basket of wings, barely touched his fries, and then teamed with Forgan for a game of pool against two others. Forgan went on a run to win it; the boy and the cop slapped high-fives in celebration.

At the family's house one night, Sue took out a piece of Charlisa's artwork to show a visitor. It was a painting that had been on exhibit in a show at a Hamilton gallery just days before she was killed. The work depicts two hands cupped over a glowing ball of energy, which represents the spirit. Eugene had seen the piece many times. But this time he stared closer, as though witnessing it for the first time. His nana had told him she could see Char's own image in the painting. And now, staring at the painting, his eyes widened, Eugene's voice grew excited, as though opening a gift on Christmas morning. For the first time, he could see her.

"There, oh, I see it now — the head, the body. She must have made it so that she's in it. There's her legs, and belly. Probably with me in it."

Charlisa had given her last work a title. She called it *Life After Death*.

The Jackie McLean homicide remains an open case with Hamilton Police. By law Carl Hall cannot be charged with her murder a second time. As for Eugene, he is now in his mid-teens. He has grown to be tall and thin, is personable, but has also got into trouble, skipping a lot of school, running away. In this Sue Ross laments that she sees some of her daughter, Charlisa, who also rebelled as a teen. Life is tough for Sue. The Zellers she worked at closed. At 60 she knows job prospects are bleak; she has planned to sell her house.

"There's no happy ending for us," she says. "That man ruined everything."

Part II

Darkness on Indian Trail

- 1 -

Even in daylight the house seems hidden, set well back from the country road called Indian Trail, cloistered among tall trees on a property next to a small cemetery. It is a long drive down the laneway, between two murky ponds. In the late day sun, it is dead silent by the house but for rustling leaves and the buzz of insects. Flies swarm aggressively, as though protecting their territory.

Her home sits on the outskirts of the hamlet of Lynden, between Ancaster and Brantford, the nearest gas station 15 kilometres away. The A-frame house seems too big and too remote for anyone to live there alone. But Audrey Gleave lived there by herself for 37 years. Audrey and her ex-husband built it 40 years ago on the 45-acre property. Its 17-foot vaulted ceilings allowed for a library balcony, but Audrey hadn't used the library much. She still enjoyed her books, but spent most of her time in front of one of two big, flat-screen TVs or her computer.

Audrey was 73, a retired high-school teacher, who, many years ago, had been a master's student in nuclear physics at McMaster University. She had always kept details of her past hidden, even from those close to her. She was an enigmatic, quiet recluse; she enjoyed her peace and privacy, although she also delighted in revving up her shiny white Camaro. She could be sociable too — for years she met for coffee every Wednesday with retired teacher friends from Westdale Secondary School. She never gave away too much of herself, though. In fact, her old colleagues never even knew that Audrey had herself attended Westdale.

The home in the country where Audrey Gleave lived.

Audrey Gleave was a retired teacher who had lived alone for years.

On Monday, December 27, 2010, the morning broke sunny and cold. Audrey had not been feeling well. She sent a couple of emails. One, to Linda, a neighbour across the street, whom Audrey knew but had never welcomed inside the house. She sent the same email to Phil, a 22-year-old McMaster University engineering graduate student who did small jobs around the house and property for her. Audrey always shared jokes, articles, and videos by email. But this one was different. It was a concert rendition of a spiritual hymn. She was not a religious person, though, and never forwarded songs.

Phil had recently erected a new mailbox at the end of Audrey's driveway. Someone had knocked down the last one. Phil was a rare acquaintance she welcomed inside her home. They would sit on the sofa and chat. He called her "Aud." No matter how many times he visited, though, Phil never seemed to be accepted by Audrey's dogs. Two German shepherds, they were so protective they would circle her as though forming a wall, barking and nipping..

Later that day, she sent a new email, to Phil:

> Monday, Dec. 27, 2010, 10:46 a.m.
> Subject: report
> From: baryon@golden.net
> By Sunday the weakness was disappearing but still there. And would you believe that this morning I got a secondary infection; runny nose, runny eyes, sneezing. But at least I don't feel weak so don't think I've a fever. I'm just annoyed with it. Hope it gets better because I intend to have coffee Wed. come hell or high water. I've got cabin fever. Lynne is coming over with soup in a few minutes.
> Bary

Bary was not her real name. It was short for Baryon, a name she had chosen for herself. It was a name that inevitably aroused curiosity in others. When Audrey had taken computer studies at Mohawk College in her sixties, a fellow mature student in her class, a man named John Hartig, noticed that she signed her assignments with that name. *Unusual*, he thought.

Hartig also noticed that she seemed to keep to herself, immersing herself in her studies. Computers had become Audrey's latest enthusiasm. She plunged into a new area of interest stoked by a natural curiosity, competitiveness, and a big analytical brain. She often stayed after class to soak up additional wisdom from instructors.

Most of the students were much younger, but she was sharper than all of them. She became a computer whiz, ultimately asking a friend to email her viruses so she could study them, break them down. She received a grade of 99 percent in one computer course. When she asked the instructor what her one mistake had been, the instructor couldn't point to one specifically, but observed that nobody knows the material perfectly, so there had to be an error somewhere. Audrey knew better. She took the complaint to the head of the department and got her 100 percent.

One day Hartig held a door open for her. It looked as if she was in pain when she walked; perhaps because she was overweight, he thought. Her knees must be hurting. He wondered if his chivalry had endeared him to her, because she spoke to him a bit. That's when he asked about the code name.

"Do you know what Baryon means?" she asked, quizzing him, no doubt certain he would have no answer.

"It's a subatomic particle," he said.

That was correct. He figured she was impressed by that, even though it was not the full definition, which would have been elementary for Audrey. (Baryon: a subatomic particle with a mass greater than or equal to that of the proton, composed of three quarks; from the Greek *barus*, meaning heavy.) Audrey emailed John after that; sent him articles, cartoons from the comic strip *Crabby Road* featuring a character named Maxine, a wisecracking, curmudgeonly elderly woman.

John was a wedding photographer. He asked Audrey for scripting tips when creating his website and credited her on the site when it was complete. He liked and respected her. He also knew that she was rather guarded. He got the impression that, while she had a big heart, she chose her friends judiciously and had little patience for those who were lazy or hypocritical, and that she felt that there was no shortage of such people.

He was one of several people on her email contact list. She emailed each person separately, never as a group. It was a privacy thing. More unusual was Audrey's insistence that anyone emailing refer to her as Baryon, or Bary, even within the text of a message. She made it clear if anyone wrote her real first name, at any time, they would be cut off.

Not long after Christmas, Hartig came home from a vacation. He saw on the TV news that an elderly woman who lived alone in the country with two dogs had been stabbed, murdered in her home. The victim's name appeared on the screen.

"My goodness," John said to his wife, feeling his heart drop. "That's Baryon."

II

"Horrendous," said the plainclothes staff sergeant. "Savage."

Steve Hrab had recently turned 59, and was nearing the end of a high-profile and sometimes controversial career with Hamilton Police. Hrab had helped send cold-blooded killers to jail. Sometimes his investigative techniques and aggressive approach had also landed him in hot water with supervisors, judges, and defence lawyers. He had seen it all, investigating homicide cases for 25 years, longer than any active Hamilton police officer. Yet he spoke to the media with pronounced gravity about the murder of the 73-year-old woman on Indian Trail. He said it was the worst thing he had ever seen. The attack had had a "sexual component," he added.

Homicide investigators typically speak to the media about an open case in the interest of public safety — he urged residents in the area to "be vigilant," since a killer was at large — and in the hopes of encouraging tips, and, on occasion, to spark a reaction from the perpetrator.

Audrey Gleave's body was found mid-morning on Thursday, December 30. Hrab said they suspected a random attack by a stranger. Police did not reveal the exact time of death, if they were aware of it. The last time she was known to be alive was the early evening of December 27. Her body was found in her garage, which was attached to the house. Audrey's two German shepherds had been inside the house, apparently unable to save her.

Hrab did not reveal additional pieces of the picture, details only the killer would know, what investigators call "holdback evidence." He spoke of a vicious stabbing but did not talk about other weapons (at least one other had been used), or the nature of the "sexual component" — it had included a perverse act that went beyond a conventional assault; the killer had taken something from the victim, as though making off with a souvenir.

Hrab stood in a topcoat against a cold wind, addressing reporters on Indian Trail, yellow crime scene tape hanging from Audrey Gleave's new mailbox.

"Have you been in contact with a man neighbours say has been doing odd jobs for Ms. Gleave?" asked a reporter from the local television station. The reporter was talking about Audrey's friend, Phil Kinsman. He lived in west Hamilton, about a 20-minute drive away. Neighbours called him her handyman.

"Yes, we have spoken with that individual," Hrab said. "He is actually the individual that discovered her. He has been ruled out as a suspect in this, absolutely."

"Neighbours say they have seen a homeless man in an abandoned barn down the road," the reporter continued, "sometimes with his shirt off, carrying an axe, and that he's been arrested and is in Brantford. What can you confirm about those reports?"

"I am aware of a homeless man that has taken residence up there," Hrab said. "We are aware he has been arrested in Brantford on a totally unrelated matter. On a weapons charge, I believe."

Hamilton police officers executed search warrants on Audrey's home and the barn six kilometres away. They did not report finding any items stolen from the house.

The sexual assault and murder of an older woman in her home was a story in the media across the country. Soon after the news broke, the phone rang at the home of David Gleave in British Columbia. It was his brother, Allan, on the line. Allan Gleave was Audrey's ex-husband. To David, Allan did not sound upset; the voice was matter-of-fact. But then Allan had not been in touch with her for many years.

"Did you hear the news about Audrey?" Allan asked.

Allan had not been contacted by Hamilton detectives about the murder. Police would not call Audrey's ex-husband for five months. Instead, he had heard the news when a *Hamilton Spectator* reporter had called him. Unlike his brother, David had been in touch with

Audrey in recent years. He remembered something she had once told him. Audrey had said she feared that she would one day be raped and murdered in her home.

When her life began, she was Otte Wilma Doveika, born in Hamilton on February 6, 1937. Her parents were from the Baltics, Latvia and Lithuania; their anglicized names in Canada became Antanas (Tony) and Marie Doveika. Tony Doveika worked in Hamilton as an engineer for Greening Wire Company. He married Marie and they moved to 179 Locke Street North, and then to 19 Mulberry Street, downtown. Otte changed her name to Audrey as a teenager. She did not get along with her mother; they barely talked.

By 1960 Tony had moved the family to 11 Beulah Avenue, off Aberdeen Avenue, near Dundurn Street. By the time she was 23, Audrey was working as a clerk at Bell, and in 1964 was enrolled in science at McMaster University. In first year at McMaster, she met Allan Gleave, who was six years her junior and studying engineering. Allan had attended Hill Park Secondary School; his father was a purchasing agent for Firestone, and his uncle, also named Allan, was a Hamilton police officer.

Allan found Audrey attractive. She was full-figured and in good shape, with long hair she usually coloured red. Most appealingly, she had a sharp wit fuelled by her intelligence.

"She read only two magazines," quipped Allan. "One was *Scientific American* and the other *MAD* magazine."

She was also a private woman, who volunteered little about her past. Maybe that was because she was older than her peers, or perhaps something had happened to her as a young woman that inspired such caution. Whatever it was that led Audrey to form a protective shell, it would remain for the rest of her life.

One day Allan spotted an old elementary school science textbook of Audrey's. He opened the front cover. There it was, handwritten: Otte Wilma. She had never told him her original name. He made a mental note about that textbook. It had been an old book, all right — had to be, he reflected, because the element tungsten was still referred to by its old name: wolfram.

Hamilton Spectator.

Young Audrey Doveika before she was Audrey Gleave.

They seemed a good match, Allan and Audrey. They decided to get married, but Allan was Anglican and his church would not perform the service. The reason? His fiancée had been married before. Twice. Audrey confirmed the two previous marriages, but would tell Allan little about them. Allan never asked her much about it. He knew better than to try; she was too private. She did not tell him she had been just 16 when she first married. That one had not lasted long. The second, which took place when she was in her twenties, was to Larry Blake, who worked at Stelco.

Even with the secrecy, Allan loved being with Audrey; she was fun and smart. They were married in 1969 in the Salvation Army chapel on James Street North. Only a couple of people attended; Allan's mom, Marjorie, threw a party for them afterward. They lived for a time with Allan's parents. Marjorie got along well with Audrey, although she dreaded family gatherings with Audrey's parents. Tony Doveika liked his booze, especially when socializing, and insisted on getting Marjorie's husband drunk every time they got together.

Before getting married Audrey had been on track for a career in nuclear physics — an uncommon vocation for a woman in the 1960s. She graduated with a bachelor of science in 1966 from McMaster and began work on a master's degree in physics. She worked two summers for Atomic Energy of Canada at the nuclear laboratories in Chalk River, 180 kilometres west of Ottawa. A densely academic article published in 1967 lists "A. Doveika" as one of the authors. The title: "Compendium of Thermal Neutron Capture Ray Measurements."

In August 1967 she was featured in a *Hamilton Spectator* article headlined COLOUR TV SET EASY TO BUILD. It was in the early days of colour television, when a new one cost a small fortune — $1,200, or about $8,000 in today's dollars. Audrey had sent away for parts and put it together over the course of a month, following a manual. She was described in the article as a "cheerful blonde brandishing her soldering iron … glibly reeling off technical terms" as her Siamese cat, Ming, watched. She was quoted as saying that anyone could put a TV together: "Anyone who has the courage to pick up a screwdriver. That's the beauty of it. Just read the instructions."

She added that she had a practical reason for building her own TV: "Now I can make my own repairs." A photo with the story showed Audrey working on her invention in a striped dress, a ring on her wedding finger. She used to wear one, even though she was single at the time. Sometimes she wore a gold snake ring. Why she did that, Allan was never sure.

Her career as a nuclear physicist did not pan out, either by choice or necessity. One family member said she was denied a permanent job at Chalk River because of management's concerns about the consequences of her working in a nuclear energy environment if she were to become pregnant. She did not complete her master's program. Instead, she announced to Allan one day she would teach high-school science. There was no discussion about her reasons. Her first school was Hill Park; later she moved to Barton Secondary, and then Westdale.

Her parents moved to 93 South Oval in Westdale. Audrey continued to be estranged from her mother, even as she worked just around the corner from her parents' house. Early in their marriage, Allan and Audrey lived on Alma Lane in Ancaster, then built a big home on Indian Trail, which Allan designed.

There were good times. Allan's brother, David, was a pilot, and flew the two of them up north into the bush to camp for a week. They travelled to Europe for three weeks. She talked about having kids. In 1974, when Allan was 31 and Audrey 38, the marriage started to fall apart. Allan had met a younger woman at his karate class. Allan's mother, Marjorie, who is now 95 and lives in a Hamilton nursing home, lamented the end of the marriage: "Men don't like women who are smarter than they are."

Allan left Audrey, but on occasion he still dropped by Indian Trail to help with things. Despite the fact that they seemed to have maintained a friendship, Audrey started referring to him in conversation as Fartface, a nickname that would have resonated with Maxine, the crusty cartoon character she had come to admire. Allan moved 400 kilometres away with the woman he had met in karate class and would marry. He settled up north, taking a chemical engineering job for a paper company in Sturgeon Falls. He never had kids and retired in 2001.

In the divorce settlement, Allan signed the house over to Audrey. The house was important to both of them, and he didn't want anyone else to live there. "I'll never sell it," she told him.

Audrey remained on Indian Trail, alone. Allan made trips back to Hamilton each year to visit his parents. When his father died in 1976, Audrey attended the funeral and chatted briefly with Allan. It was the last time they ever spoke.

III

Staff Sergeant Steve Hrab addressed reporters on Thursday, February 10. It was a big day.

"To put together a case, there are two ingredients," he said. "There are witnesses, and there are forensic pieces of evidence. In combining those two, we do our best to identify an individual, and turn him from a suspect into a person that we believe we have the necessary legal requirements, namely the grounds to arrest and successfully prosecute.

"We were able to do that yesterday."

Little over a month had passed since Audrey Gleave had been killed. Hrab, case manager of the investigation, was announcing an arrest. Detectives Paul Johnson and Angela Abrams had also been working on the case. Earlier that day Hamilton Police officers had arrested David Scott at a laundromat in Brantford. He was charged with first-degree murder, meaning the murder was planned and/or involved a sexual assault.

He had been targeted as a person of interest early in the investigation. Described as a 50-year-old homeless man who squatted in a barn near the victim's home, Scott had been charged for breaching probation by carrying a hunting knife in Brantford on December 29 — the day before the body was found with extensive stab wounds. Hrab said witnesses had seen him in the area of Audrey's home.

During the proceedings dealing with the breached probation matter, a Brantford judge opined in court that he believed David Scott was not violent, but that he could be intimidating because he frequently yelled in public places. The *Brantford Expositor* reported that he had been previously convicted for assault and cruelty to animals, and that he was schizophrenic. The day after his release from the Brantford jail on the previous offence, Hamilton police packed him off to Barton Street jail.

Meanwhile, investigators waited for evidence collected at the murder scene, Audrey's house, and the barn to be tested at the Centre of Forensic Sciences in Toronto. Police would not describe the nature of the forensics, however. Fingerprints? DNA? A footwear impression at the scene or on the victim? They wouldn't say.

There was a question as to whether Scott fitted the killer's profile. When homicide detectives search for a killer, they sometimes request a profile be developed by the Ontario Provincial Police Behavioural Sciences Section. Steve Hrab had taken courses in criminal profiling, the science of studying behaviour to paint a portrait of the perpetrator, which can assist in identifying a suspect. He placed stock in its use as an investigative tool.

Perhaps a profile seemed unnecessary in this case, since David Scott appeared to be a slam-dunk suspect: previous arrests; known in Brantford for unpredictable behaviour; seen carrying a large knife; and spotted near the victim's home. But a behavioural profile of the killer in the Gleave case likely would have suggested the perpetrator was a younger male, in his twenties or early thirties, and someone who had known Audrey, or known of her, which was not the case with David Scott.

"[The killer] has knowledge that an elderly female lives there by herself," said Mark Safarik, a retired FBI profiler with expertise in violent crime against the elderly. Safarik said those who kill the elderly "are not opportunistic offenders. They are not breaking into a place and stumbling upon the victim. He knows she's there, know she's by herself, and he goes there with intent to sexually assault and murder her. This is different than prior research suggesting women were opportunistic victims of non-violent offenders who become violent at the scene."

These are angry young men with pent-up rage toward women; they likely live with a female authority figure, he said. They are socially incompetent and feel that they have little control in their lives; they are typically undereducated, have substance abuse problems, and are unemployed or in a menial job. "For these guys, there is not a lot of planning, and they don't stay at the scene long. They leave evidence, don't clean up. They don't think that far ahead."

Another identifying sign is that they typically use far more violence than necessary to kill. Overkill is indicative of their anger. This had been the case on Indian Trail. They attack elderly women because they are easy targets — a child does not present as ready a victim because he is seen as having guardianship, whereas an elderly woman on her own has none. These killers also tend to live relatively close to their victim.

"But a homeless guy in his forties or fifties?" Safarik asked rhetorically when considering the Gleave case. "Hmm.... My advice is look young and look close."

Steve Hrab neared the end of his news conference in which he had announced that police had the evidence to send David Scott to prison for life. Then he added: "I would hope that if the public has any information about Mr. Scott, please call us."

Someone from the public did call. Her name was Debbie and she lived in Brantford. She was David Scott's sister.

"You've got the wrong guy," she said.

– IV –

"Don't let aging get you down. It's too hard to get back up!"

"I've still got 'it' but nobody wants to see it!"

"Ever notice the ones who tell you to calm down are the ones who got you mad in the first place?"

Audrey Gleave emailed these *Crabby Road* comics to a friend at four o'clock one morning. Her affection for Maxine, the cantankerous protagonist in the comic, perhaps reflected the ups and downs over the course of her life. No doubt Audrey, a deep thinker, had often wondered how things might have gone differently. She had married the wrong man — three times. She had had a career as a high-school science teacher, but could well have become a renowned nuclear physicist. Through middle age she was in good shape physically, played tennis and golfed, but in the final years of her life, her health was not the best. She smoked and lamented putting on weight in the winter. She often wore stretchy pants that she was always hitching up; a pack of cigarettes could usually be seen bulging in the back pocket.

When she taught at Hill Park, Barton and Westdale secondary schools, Audrey was known for her quirky sense of humour. She kept a picture of Albert Einstein in class and called him "my boyfriend." She handed out pens to students inscribed with phrases such as "physics is phun," "black holes are out of sight," and "cryogenics is cool." In the school yearbook, she was quoted in a caption under her picture: "Broaden your horizons and keep smiling, stupid."

Some called her "Mama Gleave," likely in an endearing way, although it also probably reflected her old-school discipline. One student remembered getting chewed out by her in the hall for holding hands with her boyfriend, which was against the rules. Audrey told her former brother-in-law, David Gleave, about the time an argument with a female student got out of hand at Barton. The girl told Audrey she was going to kill her and was suspended for the outburst.

In her leisure time, Audrey played golf at Brantford Golf & Country Club, and she also became a competitive bridge player. Her name appeared in the *Spectator*'s Hamilton Bridge Club results. Other players knew she was kind, and highly intelligent, if quirky. She told them how she had once built her own TV set, about how she would often stay up very late into the night working on her computer, and sleep away much of the day.

Audrey retired from teaching in 1997 at the age of 60. She started meeting with a group of former colleagues every Wednesday for coffee, first at the Williams coffee shop across from McMaster University, and later at the one on the waterfront. She visited the local Lynden library at least once a week, but most of her time was spent alone in the house on Indian Trail with her dogs, Togi and Schatze (a short form of *Schatzen*, which was German for "treasure," she said.) She had an invisible fence installed; the dogs wore collars with transmitters that kept them inside the boundaries.

She had always owned German shepherds — for protection and because she liked the breed. She had had two of her earlier dogs, Taggi and Alix, buried in Plot 106 in the Ancaster Pet Cemetery, run by Dudley Collins, her long-time veterinarian and friend. On the stone she had engraved: "My Best Friends." She often visited the plot and told friends that, when she died, she wanted her ashes buried next to her dogs.

Living alone out on Indian Trail, she would occasionally have coffee and chat with a neighbour — but always outside her house, on a bench, hardly ever inside. David Gleave said she didn't think the house was neat enough to invite guests in. And, in fact, friends who had made it inside said her house was always cluttered.

Into her late sixties and early seventies, she stopped playing competitive bridge. Her bridge mates wondered if she preferred playing alone on her computer, given her odd sleeping hours. It might have been that bridge perhaps no longer fitted with other enthusiasms, which included Sudoku, sketching, handwriting analysis, and watching her big-screen TVs. Her favourite show was *The Big Bang Theory*, a sitcom with characters that included genius physicists/geeks who interact with a waitress and aspiring actress. In 2007, Hollywood came to Indian Trail to film scenes for a B movie called *Cyborg Soldier*. Audrey delighted in having her picture taken with the movie co-star, Tiffani Thiessen, known to pop-culture junkies for playing teenage roles in the TV shows *Saved by the Bell* and *Beverly Hills 90210*.

Despite the fact that she lived alone, and had a generous teacher's pension and no children to support, Audrey always seemed to stay home, never took vacations. She eventually bought air-conditioning for the house but hated turning it on. Sometimes she lined her windows with tin foil to block the sun's rays and conserve power. Still, she allowed herself some indulgences: a riding lawn mower, the flat-screen TVs, and a new, wall-mounted convection oven, one she likely never had the chance to use.

And then there was the car. Neighbours thought she had a thing for sports cars. When she was first teaching and still married to Allan, she drove their Rover, a British model that Allan took up north with him when he left. But she had never owned anything like her pride and joy: a new white Camaro with a black stripe, the latest model of the iconic muscle car that had first gone into production in the spring of 2009.

Low-key, reclusive Audrey delighted in taking the dogs — "my puppies," she called them — for a drive, revving up the big engine and turning heads. She once drove a friend through a quiet neighbourhood in Brantford. An elderly woman on the sidewalk looked on in disgust as the Camaro rumbled past. Audrey loved it.

She had few friends. There were some, though. Lynne Vanstone was a long-time friend. She golfed in Brantford with Audrey for years; they often had coffee; and Audrey spent some time with Lynne's family. In 2007 Audrey decided it was time to write her will and made Lynne the executor.

But the one who perhaps spent the most time with Audrey was Phil Kinsman. Phil was polite and radiated an earnest, eager-to-please vibe. Phil had met Audrey four years earlier, in 2006, when he was 18 and in his first year at McMaster. He used to work at Windmill Power Equipment in Dundas. Audrey frequented the place and let it be known she needed someone to help her around her property. Phil needed the extra money, and her place was near: back then, before he got married, he lived with his parents in Brantford, just a five-minute drive away from Audrey's. So Phil gave it a shot. Things worked out well, and Phil continued to do odd jobs for Audrey. They became friends, and when Phil got married in June 2010, to a petite, attractive woman named Alex, whom he had met at church, he convinced Audrey to attend the wedding.

At first Phil had found it tough dropping by Audrey's because she talked ... a lot. The smallest job would take him several hours because she wanted to chat, educate him on all manner of things, including the intricacies of the invasive garlic mustard plant. But Audrey grew on him. He came to enjoy her quirks, looked forward to the routine of helping with a small job and chatting. The two of them shared a passion for science, although they didn't talk a lot about it. Phil had entered graduate studies in electrical and biomedical engineering at McMaster, and was working toward his doctorate. He had received a scholarship and been named valedictorian of his engineering class. He had two papers published: one was called "Dynamic binary translation to a reconfigurable target for on-the-fly acceleration," which involved applications for diagnostic imaging in medicine. He gave a bound copy of the paper to Audrey as a gift. She was delighted with the gesture and invited him over to talk about his work.

He received regular emails from Audrey, often at odd hours, at least 2,000 over the course of a few years — Maxine comics, educational articles and videos, corny jokes. She emailed Phil photos she had taken of him working in her yard, as well as cooking articles for him to pass along to Alex, who was a pastry chef at a French restaurant in Dundas. If Phil was out for dinner at a fancy place, she encouraged him to take photos of his food and email her the pictures. She loved gourmet foods and "creative plating," even though she didn't allow herself enough time to embrace the hobby. Instead, her idea of a perfect meal at home was a chicken pot pie from Costco.

There were even some adventures the two shared. Phil enjoyed telling the story of the time he fixed Audrey's mailbox. In the fall of 2010, vandals had busted up her old one at the end of the laneway. She

Hamilton Spectator/Facebook.

Phil Kinsman insisted that Audrey come to his wedding.

was livid. She bought a new mailbox, and when she discovered that a part was missing, she recruited Phil to drive with her to the hardware store. Audrey found the spare part on a shelf and stuffed it inside her big parka. She had Phil run interference, make sure no one was watching, and they scurried out the door. All this, even though she could have simply asked for the part at the counter.

Although Phil felt that he and Audrey had become close friends, however, not once in all the times he was in the house did she ever serve him coffee or watch TV with him. They would always chat on the same couch, just outside the kitchen. She would either shut Togi and Schatze in a large kennel crate she kept in the house, or urge them to be nice to Phil. When he visited, Phil would push the number code on the keypad outside the automatic garage door, meet her in the garage, and then chat with her, either inside or out. That was the routine.

On December 22, 2010, Audrey met with her retired teacher colleagues at Williams for their regular Wednesday coffee chat. Around that same time she loaded Togi and Schatze in the Camaro and visited veterinarian Dudley Collins in Ancaster to pick up vitamins for the shepherds. She let the dogs run on his property as usual and gave him a hug when she left, as she often did.

That Christmas she had felt under the weather. On Monday morning, December 27, Audrey emailed Phil and declared she would make her Wednesday coffee meeting come hell or high water. Lynne Vanstone brought her soup. Later that day, at about 6:00 p.m., she emailed a friend, Linda. She forwarded Linda the same music video she had sent Phil that morning.

Just after 2:00 a.m., Wednesday, December 29, a big, male chocolate Labrador living on a property across the road from Audrey's barked wildly, although that was not entirely unusual for the dog. Later that morning Audrey did not make her regular coffee gathering.

Just after midnight on Thursday, December 30, fog hung in the darkness over the snow-covered ground. Then it turned to freezing fog, which, as Audrey would have known better than most, occurs when water droplets supercool and freeze on contact with a surface.

Later that morning it rained. Phil Kinsman spoke to a writer from the *Hamilton Spectator*, relating his experience of what happened to him that morning. He had hesitated to talk about it with friends and classmates. Everyone wanted to share a theory about the mystery, ask him what he knew. It bothered him. He wanted to talk about Audrey's life, not her death.

"Obviously, I want to see justice served, but I don't need that to happen to have closure; I don't need to have a theory," he said. He agreed to meet the writer — at Williams, he suggested — the same coffee shop near McMaster that Audrey had frequented.

On the morning of December 30, Phil said, he drove with his wife, Alex, from their apartment in west Hamilton to Quatrefoil, the restaurant where she worked. After dropping her off, he headed to Audrey's. He turned his silver 2002 Hyundai Accent off Indian Trail into the driveway, past the small pond on the right and larger one on the left, and parked on the far side as he always did. He was bringing her a piece of her favourite cake. It was about 11:00 a.m. He did not go to Audrey's front door. He always entered through the garage. He carried the cake from his car to the twin automatic garage doors outside. He punched in the code on the keypad. The door rose. The Camaro was parked in its usual spot, both its doors closed.

That's when he saw her, he said, on the garage floor, lying on her back. Had Audrey slipped and fallen on some ice, he wondered? Up close, he saw that that was not the case.

She was wearing her winter coat. Her comfortable stretch pants were ripped. He went outside, put the cake back in the car, and called 911 on his cell. The person on the other end asked him to confirm that she was dead. He said he returned to the garage, knelt down, and felt her pulse. Then he went outside, sat on the bumper of his car, and waited.

Police spoke of the brutality of the murder, that it had been a stabbing. She had also been beaten. From what Phil saw, or remembered, it was not a gruesome scene. But it all kind of blurred over in his mind's eye. He did have flashbacks in the months to come. It messed him up. Audrey's dark eyes had been wide open, as though she was looking at him. The eyes stayed with him for a long time.

V

There was no immediate family at the memorial service for Audrey Gleave, which took place shortly after her death. She had none. Former students and friends posted loving comments about her on the funeral home website. She was an original, brilliant, funny, eccentric. She could also be a polarizing figure as a teacher. A former student, Steve Mihalich, who was in her physics class in the mid-1970s at Barton Secondary School, said she was a tough marker, and especially severe with male students. He said her expectations were high — higher than her students were able to achieve.

"It's so sad what happened to her," he said. "You never imagine that someone you knew in your past would have their life end that way."

Allan Gleave did not make the trip from where he lived up north to attend the memorial. Audrey's ex-husband had heard it was a private affair and wasn't sure he'd be welcome. And he wasn't keen on tackling the winter roads.

Two people spoke at the service. One was Phil Kinsman. His voice broke as he spoke: "I know *private* is a word that has often been used to describe Audrey, but I'm amazed at how many people she affected in her life.

"I want to share one small story. I remember the first time Audrey ever hugged me. Understand, she was a private person, but even more so with physical affection.

"I remember I was over at her house; we had spent the entire day planting flowers. She loved flowers. She shared with me all the research she had done. At the end of day, we were both exhausted and a bit frustrated, and she said to me point blank, 'Well, did you learn something today or not?' And I said, 'Of course I did.'

"The way she left us is tragic, but in these situations of chaos, it's instinctive to ask why, to look for answers. I prefer to just be so thankful she left us with a lesson, that our time is so short. Every moment we can spend together in love, and cherish together, it's so important to do that."

The other speaker at the memorial was Lynne Vanstone, whom Audrey had appointed in her will as trustee. (The will listed her house at a net value of $425,000, and personal property at $50,622.87.) Lynne handled all the arrangements. She could not fulfill Audrey's request to bury her ashes in the pet cemetery beside two of her previous German shepherds — that is illegal in Ontario. Friends said the ashes were sprinkled on the golf course in Brantford instead.

Her beloved dogs, Togi and Schatze, were assessed by animal control officials to see if they had suffered trauma during the murder. Audrey had previously purchased two plots for the dogs for when they died. A dog-loving couple out in the country adopted the shepherds.

Lynne Vanstone talked to reporters initially, but then she stopped. The whole thing had been awful, the entire experience just terrible, she said. She was too upset to talk anymore. Moreover, the killer was still out there.

"She was kind of a mystery woman," Lynne said at the memorial. "She had a positive influence on every life she touched. She was private. And caring, kind, shy at times. Chatty when you got to know her. Stubborn. Fair. Real. A beautiful mind. A kind soul. Extremely intelligent. Funny. Eccentric. Generous. Giving. There are not enough words to properly describe our Audrey. She was unique and very special."

The mystery surrounding Audrey, and her death, fuelled interest far and wide. Why was she targeted? Why was nothing stolen? One rumour was that Audrey's purse had been found by police inside the house, stuffed with important papers she always carried around, but it had been left untouched. Had the killer even entered the house from the attached garage? Were the dogs locked in the kennel inside where she kept them, or loose in the house?

Hamilton Spectator.

Phil Kinsman was emotional at Audrey's funeral.

The couple who adopted Audrey's dogs said that Togi, the big male German shepherd, was agitated every night when they tried to put him in his cage — even though the dog had spent most of his time in a cage when Audrey had him. Had the dog been trapped in his cage as Audrey was being murdered, and did the cage symbolize something frightening for him? The owner, who is a dog expert, thought that was possible.

Online true-crime chat forums discussed Audrey and the case at length. Why did she keep her married name, Gleave, all those years? Why did she not revert to her Doveika family name? Had Audrey — computer junkie that she was, up at all hours of the night — met someone online who frightened her? Is that why she was so paranoid about privacy and her safety? Had Audrey been the one to email friends just prior to her death, or was the killer on her computer, pretending to be her?

One of the oddest comments came from an American who observed — incorrectly — that Audrey's father had worked for the Atomic Energy Board in the U.S., the same place where Jack Tarrance worked. Jack Tarrance was thought by some to be the infamous "Zodiac Killer" in the San Francisco area in the late 1960s.

Others were intrigued by the fact that Audrey's parents were from eastern Europe, and by the fact that Audrey had posted a picture of Einstein in her classroom. Einstein left Nazi Germany in 1933, "only four years before Ms. Gleave's birth," wrote one commentator. "I have to wonder if there could have been some family or professional connection between Einstein and her parents."

Shortly after Audrey was murdered, word spread that the prime suspect was David Scott, the homeless man who had lived in a barn near the crime scene. His sister, Deb, visited him at the Brantford Jail in the days after the murder. David was serving time for breach of probation — he was caught with a large hunting knife concealed in his waistband when he used a washroom in a bank. Hamilton police waited for his release from the jail before they went after him and arrested him at a laundromat.

Deb looked at David, into the deep blue eyes that matched her own.

"Dave," she told him, "you might want to think about getting a lawyer. You're under investigation for Ms. Audrey Gleave's murder."

"Who?"

That was his first reaction: Who? He got upset. He told Deb maybe he knew someone who had been out that way. Why, he wondered, didn't the police come and talk to him; he might be able to help. The naïveté, the innocence in his words — Deb knew her brother had done nothing wrong and that he was not capable of such violence.

A friend pointed out to Deb that, while David was no dummy, he would not be smart enough to cover his tracks after a stabbing. Presumably, there had been blood all over the place, along with his DNA.

She had always looked out for David. He once called her his "anchor," the one person he always could count on. But if he had done it, if David Scott had killed Audrey Gleave, Deb would never try to protect him. She was sure of that.

She entertained the theory; she searched her heart. No way he had it in him to do it. She even called Hamilton Police to tell them so. The police weren't listening to Deb, though. They had their man. She knew they had zeroed in on David from the start. She read in the *Spectator* how a neighbour of Audrey's had called police offering more information, but the police had not even followed up. The writing had been on the wall. In the media, her brother was referred to as "David Laurie Scott," the use of his formal full name casting an ominous shadow.

Hamilton homicide detectives put him through an intensive interrogation. It is what detectives do: wear down a suspect until the truth emerges. He kept saying he was innocent. They showed David some pictures from the crime scene — also a common tactic. *Look at this — see this? See what was done to Audrey?*

Deb had first heard about the murder from her older brother, who saw the news on TV. And David? His name was mentioned in the media from the get-go as a person of interest: the homeless guy, a drifter who had been spotted not far from Audrey's place. Deb knew David had spent time out Lynden way, but not recently. But then she heard he had, in fact, been staying out in the barn on Lynden Road. Not good. And then he got arrested for breach of probation, carrying the knife. Also not good. The media made it sound as if David had been squatting in the barn, which wasn't the case, Deb said. He knew the woman who owned the land there. She was fine with him staying in the barn.

David Scott had grown up on a farm in Lynden, along with Deb and two brothers. He was the second born. The farm had crops, dairy; everyone worked it. When the parents split, they sold the farm; their father moved out east, their mother to Brantford. It was a tough time. Of all of them, David had loved the farm most.

From that point on, David lived a freewheeling life, without a home. He had attended Brantford Collegiate Institute, but quit. Deb always left her door open for him, but mostly he was out on the street. He gambled a bit at Casino Brantford and just hung out there. He worked as a bricklayer.

He drank some, but was not a drug user, Deb said. He attended church. Rumours in the community said he had burned down a church in town, that he was violent. Deb said that that was not true.

He was unpredictable, could be loud, had resisted arrest in the past. His mother said he was diagnosed with schizophrenia years ago. She told Deb that during the Audrey Gleave investigation police had interviewed her and asked if, with his mental health issues, David's anger would sometimes escalate. She had agreed that could sometimes be the case.

Deb understood how it all looked. He was a marked man because of his proximity to the crime scene, his record, the knife, his personality.

The *Brantford Expositor* reported that David had once been arrested for cruelty to animals. Deb knew that cruelty to animals was considered a significant sign. Wasn't that part of the profile for a serial killer — hurting animals? Didn't it show that you were mentally unstable, had anger issues. And David's mother had said that she and her son had been on poor terms recently. So, perhaps people thought that he had taken it out on Audrey Gleave.

Deb said it all wasn't what it seemed. That big knife he carried — he didn't use the thing. He didn't hunt. He went into town each day to borrow a dollar from someone to buy food. He bought the knife with Christmas money his dad had sent him; showed it to the family for shock value. Cruelty to animals? She said that charge was for letting his girlfriend's cat run away on purpose because he was jealous of all the attention the pet received. David had definitely been upset around Christmastime. The family had not wanted him to come over, which Deb thought was wrong. But the situation was manageable; he could always vent to her. She knew it was not something that would push him to hurt somebody.

The *Brantford Expositor* reported that the judge who presided over the breach of probation matter portrayed David Scott as a loose cannon, but not dangerous. He has a problem with authority figures, Justice Ken Lenz said, "but the fact is, if you leave him alone, he's fine.… I know he frightens people. Sometimes he frightens me."

In February, Deb's second reaction upon hearing about her brother being charged with murder was to call police and lobby for his innocence, to wrack her brain about who might really be the killer. She thought about calling neighbours on Indian Trail herself, but wondered if they'd be freaked out hearing from "the murderer's sister." Her first reaction upon hearing the news was to slide off her chair, roll into a fetal position, and weep for a long time. She knew that if David was sent to jail he'd never survive. She talked to her dad on the phone about it.

"I've just lost my brother."

VI

"No reasonable prospect of conviction."

Those five words, spoken in court on Friday, June 3, 2011, by Hamilton assistant Crown attorney Warren Milko, kicked the Audrey Gleave murder investigation back to square one. Perhaps further back than that. "The decision to terminate a prosecution can be one of the most difficult for Crown counsel to make," Milko told Ontario Court Justice John Takach.

Milko said the threshold for determining "reasonable prospect of conviction" requires the Crown to consider availability and admissibility of evidence, credibility of witnesses, and possible defences that might be used in the case. He said that threshold had not been reached. "Accordingly, the Crown is requesting that the charge against Mr. David Scott be withdrawn."

David Scott had gone from the prime suspect headed to a trial in which he could end up imprisoned for life, to being a free man. His sister Deb was overjoyed. The entire family had been put through emotional torment for five months. She believed the police had been trying to squeeze a square peg into a round hole from the start with David. They had had tunnel vision.

Jail had been a horrible experience, David told her. He had been arrested by Hamilton Police in February and had spent some of his time in solitary confinement. He told Deb that he prayed for their family every day. When he was released from Barton Street Jail, she arrived to pick him up. The local TV news cameras were there, too. She was shocked.

"We are not a story anymore; why were they there?"

She hustled him away, the cameras followed. She threw a stone, yelled into the lens. David tried to calm her down. He was an innocent man, and now his identity was broadcast all over the Golden Horseshoe. She reacted frantically at that moment, but chuckled about her reaction later. Great optics, once again. She had lost a front tooth biting into an orange recently; she had always been very thin as well. Folks watching on TV probably thought the "murderer's sister" was some kind of hillbilly on crack, she reflected.

The day the charges were dropped, Staff Sergeant Steve Hrab, the case manager, did not talk to the media. A Hamilton Police spokesperson said he was on vacation. Another officer said the results returned from the Centre of Forensic Sciences in Toronto did not match David Scott, and so the charges were dropped. He would not say what type of forensic testing had been done.

It's not unusual for police to arrest a suspect and lay charges while still waiting for evidence to be developed — forensic or otherwise. But it is uncommon for the suspect to be freed when that evidence comes back. It was a big blow to Hamilton Police and the homicide unit. Police once again urged residents in the area to be "vigilant." A killer was still on the loose.

David Scott's lawyer, Charles Spettigue, tore a strip off Hamilton Police, accusing them of shoddy investigating and worse. "Hamilton Police arrested him and tried to build their case around him," the lawyer said on TV. "Finally they ran out of straws … they wanted a quick answer, rushed to judgment to appease the folks of Ancaster, a well-to-do suburb of Hamilton, so they grabbed the first person who was different and unique. If he lived in Ancaster and had a family pedigree and money, you can rest assured he would not be treated this way." When asked if he would take legal action against the Hamilton Police Service on behalf of his client, he said, "I'd rather not say right now."

The rule for homicide investigation is that detectives must build a mountain of evidence. They expect that in court the defence lawyers will chip away at their case, argue that the judge remove pieces of evidence from the mix, give the accused every chance at a fair trial — and then some. If the mountain is not built high enough, the Crown will lose.

Clearly, the mountain had not been built high enough, since even the Crown had declined to prosecute the case.

Hamilton homicide investigators frequently work with an assistant Crown attorney prior to laying first-degree murder charges, to outline the evidence gathered, lay out the case, and ultimately ensure the Crown is on board — that the prosecution anticipates a reasonable chance of conviction. Investigators know that it hurts their credibility with the Crown's office when they present a case light on evidence.

Why had Hamilton Police made the arrest in the first place, absent evidence in hand that was necessary to stand a solid chance of conviction at trial? Part of the reason was Steve Hrab's inclination to pursue a prime suspect aggressively. Senior officers familiar with Hrab's career say this has been his pattern. And in some respects, David Scott looked good as a suspect. Another motivating factor may have been perceived pressure from the public to arrest someone quickly.

Audrey Gleave was not someone the public could dismiss as an inner-city drug addict who wrote the end to her own story. She was a retired teacher, living on her own. The case hit too close to home. And there was the issue of public safety. If the murder had been a random one, as Hrab had speculated, and you let the prime suspect live free, he might kill another person — although surveillance might have addressed that concern, and had been used on suspects in previous murder cases.

Terri-Lynn Collings, a spokesperson for Hamilton Police, said officers would not comment on the case because the investigation was ongoing. She did say that "no one has been ruled out as a suspect."

Not long after the charges were dropped, a new case manager, Staff Sergeant Ian Matthews, was named to replace Steve Hrab. That move was "based on some competing caseloads and some court commitments," according to police spokesperson Catherine Martin.

For the renewed investigation, police went back to interviewing neighbours and friends of Audrey. Fresh eyes looked at the crime scene. Was everything as it had seemed? Might the killer have staged the scene, including the "sexual component" to throw off detectives? A behavioural profile of the killer was now requested from the OPP's profiling section. Investigators had already contacted the OPP to see if the case was linked to any others in the province. They believed it was not.

Police still did not interview Audrey's ex-husband, Allan Gleave, or her former brother-in-law, David Gleave, who had been in touch with her in recent years — although he said that he had phoned police himself offering assistance.

David Scott, who continued to rent a room in downtown Brantford, was off the hook as a suspect, but police knew that his name would never stop being associated with the case, and that it would be a factor in any future prosecution. He would always be held up in court by defence lawyers in future prosecutions as an alternative suspect, since police had clearly believed at one time he was the killer. If the case ever made it to court, they would need to prove that David Scott had not killed Audrey.

The house on Indian Trail, meanwhile, was cleared of Audrey's belongings, and purchased by a couple. In the spring Allan Gleave was in Hamilton with his wife, visiting his mother. He drove up to see the house he had designed. He couldn't believe the size of the trees they had planted long ago. It was a bit disturbing to see the house, he said. He was the one who had wanted her to stay, to never sell the place. And it upset him that someone else was soon going to be living there.

As for Phil Kinsman, he enrolled in the Ph.D. engineering program at McMaster, presented a paper at a conference in San Diego in June, and put the final touches on his master's thesis. (The subject matter: computational acceleration for medical imaging — speeding up testing for a CT scan, for example.)

He had already been interviewed by police, and ruled out as a suspect by Steve Hrab early in the investigation. But in mid-August, police asked him to take a polygraph test — a lie detector — and he agreed. A detective told him flat out that he was a person of interest. Phil understood why police were spending time with him.

"To some extent I can understand it, because I had opportunity. I gather that's all you need for them to declare you a person of interest."

For most questions, police request one-word answers during a polygraph.

"Did you kill Audrey Gleave?" he was asked.

"No."

"Did you cause her physical harm?"

"No."

"Do you know who killed Audrey?"

"No."

"Were you present when she died?"

"No."

Phil asked the detectives some questions of his own. Were they talking to other persons of interest? "That's one question they would not answer for me," he said. "It's frustrating, because they share so little information but they expect so much."

In September 2011 he met with police again for more questions, to address what they called "discrepancies" in his polygraph.

Audrey, always the smartest one in the room, a woman with a dark sense of humour, who liked to channel the irascible comic character Maxine, might well have offered a wry joke about the whole thing, the fumbled investigation and all. If only she were still around to help solve the puzzle.

On the morning of December 27, not long before the end of her life, the snow-covered ground shimmered in the winter sun. Audrey was fed up with feeling under the weather. But that morning, instead of a Maxine joke or some techie article, she emailed a music video to a friend. And that evening she sent it again to another. It was, for her, an unusual selection. The video was a live performance by the André Rieu Orchestra. Rieu is an acclaimed Dutch conductor and performer. The performance was described as a Celtic version of the timeless spiritual hymn "Amazing Grace."

The rendition begins with a single musician playing a pennywhistle. It grows larger, Rieu on his violin, then other sections, including a bagpiper, joining in wave upon wave, until the stirring climax — the soul-shaking lament of 300 pipers and a choir singing. It brings audience members to tears.

> Amazing Grace, how sweet the sound,
> That saved a wretch like me.
> I once was lost, but now am found,
> Was blind, but now I see.

In the past couple of years, Audrey had talked more about the end of her life. And she had had that premonition, long ago, that it would end suddenly and violently. Being moved by that video, sending it to friends, was it a sign? Did the beautiful mind sense something — mortality, perhaps — approaching that bright morning, two days after Christmas? How many times did she replay the song, which is about redemption, about having the soul delivered from despair through the mercy of God?

Audrey Gleave wasn't religious, at least not by appearances. But she asked questions about faith, and was curious about all things. But then no one knew what existed behind the face she presented to the world. The rest of her life numbered mere hours after absorbing the vibrations of that song. Perhaps, when the final darkness descended, she heard its heavenly echoes, and that music, not the killer, was her final companion.

> Through many dangers, toils and snares
> I have already come;
> 'Tis Grace that brought me safe thus far
> And Grace will lead me home.

As with all homicide cases where there has been no conviction, the Audrey Gleave homicide case remains an open one. Ian Matthews remains the case manager. When asked at the time that Death's Shadow *went to print if the police were at all close to making an arrest, a spokeswoman with the Hamilton Police Service would only say that "the investigation is ongoing."*

Part III

Eternal Pain

She took her first breath on a Saturday in June and her last on a cold Wednesday in March. This is the story on the gravestone. Just 26 years passed in between — her life all prologue. An old man shuffled up the row in the cemetery, sun shining off his silver hair, moving well considering the hip and knee replacements. He remarked on how many graves had joined his daughter's over the years. His name is on the stone, too, the date of death left vacant.

A woman visited a while back, left flowers and a letter. She knew the victim not at all in life, but in death feels a connection that mystifies and haunts her. She researches the case, sits in the house where the homicide happened, and thinks of her.

A man and his two sons come to the cemetery to visit the graves where family members lie, but each time the man wanders off on his own. He does not tell his boys why it is he pauses wordlessly in Section 15, Row 25; does not reveal that he's thinking of the woman with the silky blonde hair.

The old detective does not visit. He lives up north on two acres, by cool water and tall pines. He speaks in a gravelly baritone, his face softened by a grey beard, hands still rugged and hard, the eyes deep green. He says he closed the drawer on the past when he retired. Still, on occasion, it floats into his mind's eye, the scene in that basement a long time ago. No, he does not dwell on the past. But he also does not forget that when all was said and done, he still had a case left out there.

March 29, 1978
2:30 a.m.
Hamilton, Ontario

The man held the hostage at knife-point. It was his own son. He demanded a flight out of Canada for both of them. The Hamilton detective, who was tall, with dark hair and green eyes, dressed in a jacket and tie, stood on the other side of the apartment door, speaking calmly in the deep baritone, stalling.

"It's going to take a little longer," said Don Crath. "We just need a little more time. Got to finish arrangements for the flights."

To lessen the man's tension, stall for time, Crath tried to make a connection with the man. "Do you have a picture of your son? You show me a picture of your son and I'll show you a picture of my two boys."

The man slid a photo under the door.

"Nice looking boy. You don't want to harm your boy, do you, Bill? I know you don't want to hurt anybody. I sure don't want to get any of my policemen hurt. Just hang on."

He kept the man with the knife talking for more than two hours. Then he and officers Bill McCulloch and Vern Cummins burst through the door, rescued the boy, made the arrest. The story would make headlines in the *Spectator* the next day; reporter Darryl Gibson had been listening to the whole thing.

Crath drove back to the weathered old detectives' office on King William Street, where he worked in the Criminal Investigations Division. The place was old school; cops there sat in beat-up wooden chairs and smoked, the interrogation room had flecks of blood on the wall. Known for wearing natty suits, Crath usually stood out. However, he felt rather beat-up himself that morning. He loosened his tie, rubbed his tired eyes, and typed his report as morning broke.

Crath was 41 and had started as a cop in his early twenties. That had been soon after his wife Darlene gave birth, to twin boys. He figured that policing was a solid family job, better than getting stuck on the road in sales. Turned out he liked being a cop and was good at it. Solid police work, he knew, was about trusting your gut. Keep it simple, use common sense. It usually worked.

Hamilton Spectator.

Don Crath was an old-school cop known for wearing natty suits while on the police force.

One year after the hostage case, Don Crath was blindsided. He lost his wife, the two boys their mother. Darlene died.

Mauro Iacoboni entered a bar with his cousin near Barton and Strathearn. It was November 1981. Mauro was 27, from an Italian family, his first name pronounced *Mah-ro*, with a rolling *r*. Guys at the factory where he worked didn't roll their *r*'s all that well, though. He got called Moe.

He saw her for the first time in the bar and was instantly attracted. She was petite, with long blonde hair — very pretty, he thought. And just his luck, she was with a woman he knew. He left his cousin, walked over, said hi, chatted with both of them, his eyes mostly on the blonde. She said her name was Trisha Roach. Moments later Mauro turned to leave.

"Where are you going?" Trisha asked. The blunt tone caught him off guard.

"I ... I have to work in the morning."

Trisha continued talking with him. By the end of the night they had exchanged phone numbers and he had learned more about her.

Trisha was 26 and lived alone in a house on Montclair Avenue, just east of Gage Park. Until recently she had shared it with her husband, Terry Paraszczuk (*Paraz-chuck*). Trisha had dated Terry at Bishop Ryan high school. where they were in the same grade. She had been crazy about him. He was handsome, a charmer, the life of the party. He was more outgoing than Trisha, who usually came across as more reserved.

Trisha's parents were Ray and Floria Roach, who had both grown up in the city's north end. Ray's father cut ice off the bay in winter and sold it year-round. Ray carried on the family business, running a delivery service called Roach Ice. Terry's parents, Michael and Maria, had Ukrainian roots; Michael worked at a hardware store, Maria in a hospital.

Trisha married Terry on August 26, 1978, at Blessed Sacrament Roman Catholic Church on a perfect summer day. She was 23. Trisha's sister, Cathy, her only sibling, was maid of honour. The sisters were close, born just 11 months apart; both were nurses. Now that his daughter was a Paraszczuk, Ray Roach carried a slip of paper in his wallet with the new name on it so he wouldn't forget the spelling.

Hamilton Spectator.

The crime scene in Trisha's house was a disaster from the fire and the water used to douse it.

Trisha and Terry bought the old red brick two-and-a-half storey house at 944 Montclair. Terry had recently started a job as a customs officer, while Trisha had worked for three years as a nurse in the neurology department at Hamilton General Hospital. She put up $10,000 of her savings toward the down payment. Terry's father, Michael, who lived just around the corner, did some work on the unfinished basement.

The couple's dating life had been stormy on occasion; marriage did not smooth the waters. Trisha, who was a small woman, less than 100 pounds, came across as quiet, but she stood up for herself. In 1981 they separated. Trisha returned to using her maiden name, Roach, but legally still carried Terry's. The house was put up for sale. Michael Paraszczuk told Trisha that he wanted to be repaid for his expenses fixing up some of the basement, which upset her. Ray Roach said Michael further served Trisha a lawsuit to recoup the money.

Toward the end of 1981, Trisha started dating Mauro Iacoboni. He played drums in a band with three of his cousins, and on their first date he picked her up in his van with the kit in the back. To Mauro, who lived with his parents, Trisha seemed mature, independent. She kept the house on Montclair immaculate. Although she was a smoker, the house usually smelled of cookies rather than cigarette smoke because she was always baking. She also knitted. She made a blanket for her mother, Floria, for Christmas in Floria's favourite powder blue. She sewed on her back porch in the sun.

Being with Trisha was just so easy, Mauro felt. She was sweet and pretty, and it just worked. He loved her long hair; on the job at the hospital she had to wear it up, but with him it was always down. They used to just relax in her house; ordered in Chinese food a lot, her favourite. Mauro got to know her parents, too. He'd kick back with Ray and watch hockey games at Trisha's house. He felt his relationship with Trisha deepen.

On New Year's Eve, 1981, his band played an all-night show at Queen's Banquet Centre on Barton Street, and she went to see him play. She fitted right in with Mauro's friends. At midnight the band paused, Trisha joined Mauro on stage and kissed him as the year turned to 1982.

Things were looking up for Trisha. She continued working at the hospital, where her co-workers and bosses loved her. She regularly attended St. John the Baptist Roman Catholic Church, and now met privately with her priest, Father Ron Cote. He asked if she had considered having her marriage to Terry annulled. She was interested and took home some reading on the topic, showed it to a friend. Trisha said she wanted to start over, get married again, and start a family. She decided that she needed to sell the house, so she started to look for an apartment. She had a dog, a large unruly Dalmatian named Jakes; she knew she wouldn't be able to keep him in an apartment, so she gave him away, returned him to the breeder. The house sold and she met with Terry on Thursday, February 25, to sign papers approving the sale.

A week later, Wednesday, March 3, Trisha looked at apartments with Floria and Cathy. She also had plans to meet her friend Sandra for coffee, but Sandra was under the weather and had to cancel. Floria planned to come to Trisha's house that night to join her for dinner. But Floria felt ill, stayed in bed instead.

Mauro worked the evening shift at American Can on the stamping production line. At his 7:30 p.m. break, he phoned Trisha. They chatted for almost a half-hour. She told him she had moved some boxes to the basement, getting ready for the move.

"I'll see you later," Mauro said, signing off.

"Okay, bye, pumpkin," she replied, and they hung up.

Pumpkin. Mauro smiled. It was a pet name he had heard Trisha call her nephew. She had never called him that. It felt good.

Late that night stars were out and it was very cold. Detective Don Crath drove around the lower city in an unmarked cruiser. Working CID meant taking on a bit of everything. Crath, his hair greying from 46 years of living and 20 on the force, was paired with Dave Matteson when the call came in after midnight. Firefighters had put out a house fire at 944 Montclair Avenue. A body was inside. At the scene, Crath, in suit and overcoat, spoke to a deputy fire chief.

"We have a dead body in the basement," the firefighter said.

The house still smoldered as the detectives moved down through the heat and charred stench to the unfinished basement. The floor was covered in water. Crath saw a woman's body, fully clothed, soaked. Her face was a bit dirty from the smoke, but she had suffered no damage from the fire. He saw a thin chord, like twine: a ligature. She likely had strangled. The ligature had also somehow ridden up from her neck to her face. Suicide? Possible, except Crath had been trained to treat every sudden death as a homicide. He grimaced. If it was a crime scene, it was a lousy one, he thought: evidence destroyed by either fire, smoke, water, or firefighters trampling through the place. He didn't blame the fire guys; they had to soak it. Montclair was a street of old homes. They could not risk fire spreading.

A couple of senior police officers arrived. Had to be suicide, one of them offered. Crath knew most hangings are suicides, but women usually don't use that method. Most use pills. The scene was odd. The fire had started in the basement, spread up to the first and second floors.

Some boxes and debris in the basement had caught fire. Crath figured an accelerant of some kind had been used. If she had committed suicide, how would she have set the fire?

Then there was the hanging. If she had hanged herself, it was an odd way to do it. She had not tried to do it from a rafter, kick a bucket. No, the ligature had broken, and one severed end was still tied to a wooden post on a wall — a joist, or fire stop, part of an unfinished wall where insulation and drywall had not been added. The joist was only about three feet off the floor. Crath knew some inmates in prison used a "low hang," tied on to bars for leverage, to kill themselves. But a woman in her own basement?

He also noted that the woman's arms lay straight at her side. He knew that after a hanging the hands are often near the neck. It was as though her arms had been placed in position. Suicide? Don Crath's gut said otherwise.

Ray Roach was led down to the morgue in Hamilton General Hospital by Crath. In the future, Hamilton would have a renovated morgue that would offer family members a tiny window through which to view a body for identification. But that was not the case with the old morgue. Ray watched an attendant wheel a gurney out in front of him. A body lay on top, covered by a sheet from head to toe.

Ray had been at home on the east Mountain with Floria when they got the call in the middle of the night that their daughter's house was on fire. Floria had called Trisha at 9:30 p.m., but no one answered. She called again later, kept trying, but eventually the signal was just busy. After receiving the news, Ray and Floria drove down to Montclair. Cathy, Trisha's sister, arrived as well. The scene was cluttered with fire and police vehicles; her sister's car was in the driveway.

Ray walked up to a uniformed police officer.

"Was there anyone in the house?" Ray asked.

"Yes. One person."

Cathy, a nurse, saw a car on the road that had a sign in the window. The coroner's car. Her body shook. There was a pounding inside her head; she felt sick.

Hamilton Spectator.

An old family photo of Ray, Floria, and their daughters Trisha and Cathy at Christmastime.

A neighbour of Trisha beckoned Cathy to come to his door. What did he want to tell her? She started to go, then her husband called for her. She joined her parents in a police cruiser. They answered questions, were taken to the police station. They entered a room and met Crath for the first time. He asked them about suicide. Absolutely not, they said. Trisha would never do it. Her life was turning around. Not a chance. He asked if there was anyone they believed would hurt Trisha. There was someone and they urged Crath to interview him.

There was no mystery to the identity of the victim in the house on Montclair, but by protocol she had to be identified by family. In the morgue the attendant drew down the sheet from the head of the body on the gurney. The attendant was supposed to reveal enough for identification, just past the eyes, nose. Instead the sheet dropped lower. And now Ray Roach saw it: the mark on his daughter's neck, a clean dark red welt. It was burned forever in his mind's eye at that moment.

"They must have strangled her," Ray said quietly in the room. "Used a telephone cord."

"No," Crath said softly in the deep voice. "That wasn't it."

Before dawn Mauro Iacoboni heard a voice, awakening him from a deep sleep. It was his dad. Mauro had come home from work after midnight, watched TV, and gone to bed.

His parents knew he was dating someone, but he had not told them a name or details. He knew that his dad, Azio, an old-school Italian and a Dofasco man, would not appreciate his son dating a recently separated woman.

"Mauro, you need to come to the door," his father said.

Mauro padded out of his room and into the front hallway on the same floor of the bungalow. Two men in suits in the doorway.

"Do you know Patricia Roach?" one of them asked.

"Yes," Mauro said.

"She died tonight. Would you come with us to answer some questions?"

He talked to the detectives in the unmarked cruiser and then down at the station.

"Do you know what she was doing last night?"

"Packing," Mauro said. "She said she had moved boxes to the basement. Her house sold, she's moving."

Mauro felt numb the entire time, and always would when recalling that night. Trisha was gone. He thought they were on the road to serious commitment, maybe even marriage. Now Trisha was dead, and he knew police were trying to determine if he had any role in her death.

Don Crath worked against time, and the grain. His bosses were calling it suicide. Trisha's family insisted it was murder. He believed the Roaches. Thursday morning, not pausing to sleep, he went after it by the book. Interview those closest to the victim. In homicides in a house, the victim knows the killer in 80 percent of cases. There had been no sign of forced entry. She must have known him. Trisha's death, and the fire, had happened sometime after 9:00 p.m., when she had answered the phone, and 11:30 p.m., when neighbours saw the house ablaze. Nothing had been stolen.

Right off the bat, Crath and Dave Matteson visited Trisha's estranged husband. Terry Paraszczuk, who was still working as a customs officer, lived with his girlfriend in a two-storey apartment above a store on Queenston Road in Stoney Creek. The detectives knocked on the door. No answer. They knocked louder. Terry finally answered. It was very early in the morning; he had been asleep. There had been a fire at the house, the detectives told him. Trisha was dead. Terry looked surprised. The detectives took him to the station, continued to question him, and the girlfriend. He said he had been with his girlfriend all night; she said the same thing.

Word spread that morning among friends of Trisha and Terry. A close friend of Terry, a man named John Pajek, who had been best man at the wedding, was awakened by the phone ringing at about 3:00 or 4:00 a.m. It was Michael Paraszczuk, Terry's father. Half asleep, John heard Terry's father's voice on the other end. The words did not make any sense to him.

"Tragedy," Michael Paraszczuk said. "Trisha's dead."

It was sometime after 7:00 a.m. when Trisha's friend Sandra received a call from Terry. She hadn't seen or talked to Terry in years; she had been in touch with Trisha only. Now Terry told Sandra that Trisha was dead. In disbelief, she hung up and dialed Trisha's number. The line was busy. She turned on the radio and heard about the fire on Montclair. *My God*, she thought, *it's really happening.*

The *Hamilton Spectator* reported that morning that police were investigating the sudden death of 26-year-old Patricia Paraszczuk. The story quoted Terry: "It came as much of a shock to me as everyone else," he said. "She was a beautiful person and she didn't deserve to die that way."

The post-mortem concluded the next day, Friday. The cause of death: strangulation by ligature hanging. The level of carbon monoxide in her body was 14 percent, consistent with that of a smoker; the ligature killed her, not smoke from the fire. There were no signs of sexual assault.

The body was delivered to Friscolanti Funeral Home on Barton Street. The *Spectator* reported a police official saying that Trisha had "been experiencing personal and family problems prior to her death."

That day Crath met with Ray, Floria, and Cathy. He told them her death was still being ruled a suicide. They were angry.

"It was not a suicide!" Floria said, nearly shouting. "You have to look harder."

At home that night, Crath continued brooding over the case, seeing the body in the basement. Nothing added up. He went to his workshop, hammered a few pieces of wood together to mirror the firestop joist construction where the torn ligature had been found. He knelt on the floor, trying to imagine how she could have strangled herself just three feet off the ground. It made no sense.

The next day he took his homemade re-enactment to Hamilton General Hospital and spoke to veteran forensic pathologist Rex Ferris. Ferris, who had a lofty reputation in the field, had had doubts about the suicide theory as well. He said they could learn more from further examination of the body.

With plans already set for the funeral visitation, police officers entered Friscolanti to take the body back, much to the horror of the funeral director, who had never seen such a thing. He refused, before permission to re-examine the body was granted by the coroner.

Crath had attended the first post-mortem, and on Sunday, March 7, four days after Trisha had died, he attended a second. Rex Ferris examined tissue behind the skin on her face. He detected bruising that could not be seen in the original autopsy. She had been struck prior to her death. It was not tramline bruising, which is caused by a cylindrical object, but it clearly had been an assault.

Crath could all but see it now. Trisha, just 98 pounds, punched in the face by her attacker, someone she knew, knocked unconscious or unable to defend herself; dragged to the basement, strangled, the scene made to look like a suicide. Killer sets house on fire to cover his tracks. Crath had seen it all, but this killer had been especially ruthless.

He had wondered if it was a spontaneous crime, an assault sparked by an argument. But the strangulation and arson concealment looked planned. The killer knew he could be connected to the crime by his association to the victim, or the location. So he had burned it up.

Many more questions than answers remained. Why would the killer tie the ligature to that joist? Why had the ligature torn and broke? Was it heat from the fire? The extra dead weight of her body when her clothes became soaking wet from the fire hoses? Why had the ligature been tight enough to kill, but still managed to slip up over her chin onto her face? Who had motive and opportunity to do it?

Hamilton Spectator.

Trisha Roach on her wedding day.

The family was at least pleased that the notion that Trisha had taken her own life had been put to rest. That was justice of a sort. But confirmation that it was a homicide also meant that there would be miles to go before Crath or the family could rest.

Back at the station, a senior colleague chided Crath. "You just had to turn it into a goddamn murder, didn't you."

Trisha was buried in Holy Sepulchre Cemetery on Tuesday, March 9, a bitter day with biting wind, blowing snow. Father Ron Cote presided over the funeral at St. John the Baptist, at Edgemont and King Street, a few blocks from the house on Montclair. Don Crath and Dave Matteson stood at the back of the church, watching who attended. Mauro Iacoboni was there; the family had asked him to attend.

The detectives took aside one of Mauro's friends after the funeral. The guy had showed up with a cup of coffee from Tim Hortons. Mauro figured his friend had looked a little too detached, nonchalant, so they questioned why he was there. Terry did not show at the visitation or funeral, nor did anyone from his family, or his friends. Crath was not surprised. He knew relations between Terry and the Roaches had been sour for a long time, and they were especially so now.

On March 16 police announced that Trisha's death had been a homicide. The next day Terry was quoted in the *Spectator*: "I knew right off the bat that it must have been a murder," he said. "There's no way in the world that she would do it herself.... She had absolutely no reason to kill herself. All she wanted to do was help people. For someone to cause so much harm to her is just amazing.... Yes I'm upset. I'm obviously very upset." He said that they had signed papers a week before her death in order to sell the house, and that it "was a very amicable" agreement.

A senior police officer was quoted saying "we have our ideas" about what might have happened. "But we're not saying anything, for obvious reasons."

Crath continued to meet and question Terry. With no one else jumping out on his radar, an ex-husband had to remain a person of interest, even though Terry continued to maintain that he had been with his girlfriend at the time Trisha was killed. He appeared to lack a strong motive as well. He had not benefited in a substantial financial way from her death. Trisha had moved her life insurance benefit to her mother after their separation.

Had he been angry about Trisha dating again? When she was killed he had been living with his girlfriend, a woman who also worked with Canada Customs. The detectives questioned friends of Terry, including John Pajek, asked him about Terry's character. John felt police were barking up the wrong tree.

They interviewed Terry's father, Michael Paraszczuk, who lived on Balmoral Avenue South, 200 metres from Trisha's house. Ray Roach said Michael had his own key to Trisha's place. Crath was told Michael had hard feelings toward Trisha as a result of her separation from his son. She had been killed before the lawsuit had been settled over his handyman expenses for doing work in the basement. (Michael and his wife eventually moved from the neighbourhood and could not be located to comment for this story. He later died, on February 18, 2012.)

The detectives revisited Mauro Iacoboni. Mauro took three weeks off work after Trisha died. He could not sleep at night; instead, he lay awake, agonizing over what had happened to Trisha, wondering what might have been. Crath returned to Mauro's workplace at American Can, questioned his supervisors. Was there any way Mauro could have left the factory for a while and come back on shift before punching out? Next to impossible. Everyone had seen him there, and he had been on the phone during his break. He could not have left until midnight, and by then Trisha was dead.

Crath and Dave Matteson met with friends of Trisha's at Mellows, a restaurant and bar at Highway 20 and Queenston Road, where she had gone on occasion. The detectives interviewed another man she had dated. It had been nothing serious, went nowhere.

Terry had suggested a theory: perhaps the killer had a connection to someone Trisha knew at the hospital where she worked? Crath looked into the hospital angle; there was nothing, and, in any case, she had been highly respected at work.

They had already canvassed the neighbourhood around Montclair Avenue. Trisha's sister, Cathy, continued to replay that night in her mind, especially the incident with the neighbour of Trisha who had asked her to come and talk. She should have gone. Maybe he had seen something: a car, someone approaching the house. If anyone had seen anything, they hadn't told the police. But then, it had been bitterly cold, and no one had been walking around. And the fire-damaged house had yielded no physical evidence.

Crath had come up empty. He interviewed everyone remotely connected to Trisha, and had given people of most interest a rough ride, leaning on them, old school, questioning them repeatedly. Everyone had an alibi. Not all were air-tight, but none could be disproved. He was not about to lay a charge on speculation. You only had one crack at a conviction.

On April 27 Hamilton Police offered a $10,000 reward for information that would solve the case. Soon after the Roaches added $15,000 to the reward. "We'd pay anything to put the person behind bars," Ray said in the *Spectator*. "It's all the savings we have, but it's not much when your daughter's life is involved."

Matteson moved on to other assignments. Crath stayed with it, putting more work into the homicide than any case in his career. Each day he took a phone call from Floria, who asked him for the latest news. She could not sleep; she would burst into tears in public on occasion. She felt as if she couldn't breathe, waiting for a break in the case. She prayed every night that someone would come forward in the neighbourhood — someone who saw something, or someone who knew the killer.

As spring weather began to set in, she could think only that the killer was walking around enjoying the warmth, while her daughter was under the ground. One day Ray visited the stone in Holy Sepulchre and saw flowers had been left with no name attached. Why? He went home and called the police. Crath, hungry for something, anything, showed up at his door, picked Ray up and bombed down the Sherman Cut en route to the cemetery, Ray white-knuckling all the way. Crath traced where the flowers had been purchased. He found the buyer. Turned out to be nothing, just a couple of Trisha's old friends.

Ultimately Crath's supervisor asked if he was not just treading water on the case. He was taken off it, and he locked the case file away in his desk. Floria continued calling. Don't forget about Trisha, she told him.

A cold case never closes. But no one was actively looking for Trisha's killer.

Crath continued working in CID, homicide, and drugs. During the last few years of his career, he closed out his old homicide cases in court while working out of the coroner's office, regularly attending autopsies as part of the job. He grew hardened to them. But when Don Crath came home from work after attending one, he would always undress in the garage and stuff a laundry bag with the clothes that smelled of formaldehyde and death.

IV

On Christmas Day for five years, 10 years, 20 years after Trisha was killed, Floria set the table for a family dinner in their little house on the east Mountain. Each time, when everyone had eaten, the plate and cutlery at one of the settings went untouched, remained sparkling clean. That was Trisha's place, still set every Christmas.

Pictures of her decorated the living-room walls: Trisha as a little girl; Trisha as a teenager; and, most prominently, a large one of her in the iconic nurse uniform, hair up under the hat. In that photo she looked so young and so mature at the same time. She had a look that said the future had no bounds. It was the photo that, every year, the Roaches put in the *Spectator* obituaries on the anniversary of her death with a write-up: "Why was she taken so young and so fair when earth held so many it better could spare. Hard was the blow that compelled us to part with our loving daughter so dear to our heart. She was taken without any warning, her going left hearts filled with pain, but although she's gone from amongst us in our hearts she will always remain."

Ray and Floria continued to visit her grave regularly. For a couple of years after she died, they would go three times a day: visit, linger, go for coffee, and return. Ray kept a shovel in the trunk of his car in winter. Each morning he shoveled a narrow pathway from the cemetery driveway up several metres to the stone.

Floria was never the same. She was a gregarious woman, more talkative than Ray, and put on a good face for others, but she was damaged inside. She and Ray lived in fear, for one thing, increasing the security in the house, making it impossible for anyone to break in. But mostly it was just missing Trisha and living in a dark hole with no answers or justice.

Cathy continued working as a nurse in orthopedics at St. Joseph's Hospital, but never recovered. Losing a sister who felt like a twin was like losing both arms. She couldn't tuck the pain away. She lamented that her young son, Michael, would never know Trisha.

When Cathy got talking about that horrible night, it would bring her down for weeks. As Michael grew older, he came to understand why his mom sometimes seemed so angry at the world when he was little, why she would often wear sunglasses to cover eyes swollen from shedding tears.

Some people wished Ray, Floria, and Cathy would move on. *Why could they not let go?* some asked. The killer had taken Trisha — why were they letting him slowly kill each of them as well? But no one could possibly understand their pain. Trisha had been ripped from their lives on purpose and no one had been held accountable. The wound was an open one, eternal; their anger had no release. The homicide investigation, stone-cold though it was, served to taunt them. It would remain forever an open case technically. Something could break. Couldn't it?

In 1996 veteran homicide detective Steve Hrab took over the file. Hrab, an abrasive personality, had worked some of Hamilton's highest profile murder investigations, and had been a lightning rod for controversy on the police service. He was quoted in the *Spectator* in March 1997 suggesting he knew the killer's identity.

"I'm confident that if certain things occur this case is solvable. Certain people have to come forward and tell the truth," Hrab said. "We know these people exist."

The story said Ray and Floria believed they knew who had killed Trisha. "I concur with what they believe," Hrab added. "The major focus goes back to one area. We feel we know what happened, but the evidence isn't there to proceed with criminal charges."

In a story marking the 25th anniversary of Trisha's death, in March 2007, Hrab sounded an even more aggressive tone, speaking directly to a person he believed knew the killer. That person, he said, is living a horrible life. "I know your living hell is continuing. The only way for it to end is to come forward. Open the door and step out of that life." Was

Hrab using provocative tactics, trying to incite a reaction? Hrab had met with the Roaches on occasion, they liked him, believed he felt their pain and would not stop trying to find justice for them.

For Floria, time was running out to see the case solved. She had been diagnosed with leukemia in the winter of 2006. They gave her three months to live. She lasted five, but finally died, aged 73. The family took her on a final trip, driving up to Winterlude in Ottawa. They saw the ice sculptures, swam in an indoor-outdoor pool. It was wonderful. In the hospital the family had a chance to say their final words. Floria, alert and feisty to the end, made sure they heard her final message.

"Don't give up on Trisha," she said. "Don't ever stop."

The violent, tragic end to Trisha's life and the mystery behind the cold case struck a chord with some outside Trisha's family. In 1982 Julie Neadles, a neighbour of the Roaches, was 16 when she came home during a spare at her high school the morning after the fire. She saw her mother at the kitchen table crying. She told her that Trisha had been murdered. Julie's parents were close friends of Ray and Floria, and Julie had gone to Trisha's wedding when she was a little girl.

For a long time after Trisha died, Julie would hear her mom and Floria talking about who Floria believed was the killer, sharing bits of information, speculation. Julie made a vow to herself: one day she would attend police college, become a detective, and try to crack the case. She didn't follow through on her vow and regrets it to this day. She still cannot let go of the case.

Jeanne Barnes was another Hamilton woman who was touched by the case. Every March she would look for the memoriam to the young nurse in the *Spectator*. She felt a connection to Trisha. Around 1996 she started dating a man named Doug. She visited his house at 944 Montclair Ave. He had bought it for a low price after the fire and fixed it up. Jeanne did not realize the significance of the address, not until she was inside the house and Doug showed her a photo. It was of Trisha Roach. Jeanne couldn't believe it. What are the chances that a new boyfriend lives in the house where Trisha died, and that he has a picture of her?

Hamilton Police Service.

Mauro Iacoboni sometimes visits Trisha's grave.

Jeanne plunged into the case, researching. She believed the answer was in that house — not physical evidence, but perhaps something else. She wanted to have a psychic visit. On March 3, 2007, she sat in the house on Montclair and wrote about how her connection to Trisha haunted her, but was drawing her "closer to the truth and perhaps even justice one day.... I sit alone in Trisha's house on the 25th anniversary of her death, the moon is full tonight. If only it could light the way to the truth."

The next day Jeanne went to the grocery store, bought some flowers and left them at the gravestone along with the note. Before long Steve Hrab came to interview Jeanne and Doug. He asked them what they knew, why they had an interest in the case. Jeanne still thinks of Trisha often.

"I really believe Trisha is using me, in a good sense, as a conduit between the past and present," she said. "The answer is out there."

V

"Did you kill her? Did you do it?"

In the years following Trisha's death, Mauro Iacoboni heard that question from people he knew, and wondered how they possibly could say that. He tried to move on after Trisha died. The Roaches invited him to many dinners, barbecues — they were great, but it made it difficult to feel like he could get on with his life. Eventually, he began declining the invitations and lost contact. Two years after Trisha died, he married, and eventually had two sons. The marriage did not age well, ending in divorce after 11 years.

A journalist showed up at his house one day, asking him about Trisha. For the first time, Mauro was told about the bruising on her face, that she had been assaulted before she was strangled. It upset him, but he wanted more answers. His anger was rekindled.

"The killer is nothing but a coward," he says. He begins talking as though addressing the one who did it. "There's no other word but coward. Coward. It wasn't a fair fight. A young woman. Ninety-eight pounds. You that tough? What's the matter with you? You don't like what I have to say? If you don't like it, come see me."

When he visits the cemetery with his two grown sons to see family plots, Mauro tells them he's just going for a walk by himself for a bit. And then he always stops at Trisha's stone. He thinks it's too sensitive a subject to talk about with them. His ex-wife, the boys' mother, had issues with his relationship with Trisha, how close they had been. His relationship with his sons has not been ideal. Talking about it all brings tears to his eyes. But he has decided it's time for them to know the truth about the pretty young woman he fell for 28 years ago, the pretty young woman who was taken away.

Others who knew Trisha moved on with their lives. Terry Paraszczuk works as a security inspector with Transport Canada. He ultimately married the woman he had been dating at the time Trisha died and they had children.

A journalist recently left him voice mails and emails; would he comment for a story about Trisha? Terry did not answer at first, then sent an email: "Hello, Mr. Wells, thank you for your email. Trisha's death was, and remains, unbearably upsetting to her family, and to me and my family as well. I have no desire to comment any further on this tragic event. Thank you. Regards, Terry Paraszczuk"

On February 18, 2012, Michael Paraszczuk, Terry's father, died at 89 in St. Joseph's Hospital in Hamilton.

Sandra, Trisha's best friend from childhood, stays in touch with the Roaches. She thinks about Trisha often, especially around her friend's birthday. She cannot believe someone did this to Trisha and has been able to live with himself all these years.

Don Crath lives up north, comes down to Hamilton on occasion to visit family. He has received a call or two from detectives over the years, seeking his thoughts about the case. Looking back he felt one suspect looked very good. And another was not beyond the realm of possibility. That was always the problem — given the lack of physical evidence, and that everyone seemed to have an alibi, he could never be sure enough to lay a charge. He was not about to let himself have tunnel vision and risk putting an innocent man in jail.

"I could never do that; could not live with myself if I did that."

After his first wife, Darlene, died, Crath remarried. Her name is Peggy; she worked in the emergency department at Hamilton General. For the first 10 years of retirement they spent time down south and at the cottage, then settled in one spot. It's a beautiful spread. Crath tends to his property, takes the tractor out of the back shed to cut the grass, keeps an old sports car in the garage to play with. He wears a lumberjack shirt and jeans, thick grey socks. On the wall in the living room is a big print of a rugged rancher.

"Yeah, I like that picture," he says. "My wife calls him the tough old cowboy."

Ray Roach, now in his eighties, visits Trisha's grave all the time. Cathy comes frequently, too. They both met there on June 11, Trisha's birthday. Cathy wants the killer to know they are not going anywhere. They will stay in touch with police and the media to keep the case alive. She vows they will not let him get comfortable, ever.

They may wait a long while for a guilty conscience to take its toll. For 28 years someone has lived with the knowledge that the defining moment of his life was killing a small woman in cold blood, trying to make it look like a suicide, then leaving her to burn. He has lived like this a long time, perhaps not comfortably, but lived all the same.

The crucifix from Trisha's casket hangs on Ray's bedroom door. He sits in his favourite chair in the living room, rubbing the armrest as he speaks, the fabric visibly worn. Trisha's nursing photo is above the TV; he looks at her every day. In summer he enjoys sitting on the front porch and watching the ball game through the window.

Ray was the quiet one, compared to Floria. But his Irish blood runs strong and he speaks proudly of his north end roots. Never expected to face something this difficult, though. "You raise a child from a baby, and, God, you … never dream of going through this. You just never know in life. You keep on hoping for the best."

He comes off as a gentle sweetheart of a man, but if one thing defines Ray Roach, it is toughness. Both his parents died within 10 months of each other when he was 19. In old age he suffered a bad fall. Never gives up though. At the cemetery he checks on blue flowers around the stone. He planted the forget-me-nots a few years ago.

"They die off in the summer but they come back every year."

He points out that one stone over from Trisha's, is Maggie Karer's. She was murdered and dismembered by the infamous killer Sam Pirrera 11 years ago. "It sure makes you wonder. The things people do to one another."

Father Ron Cote tried to tackle the notion of evil when he addressed Trisha's loved ones at the funeral on that cold day 28 years ago. Every

Ray Roach looks at Trisha's picture on the wall every day as he sits in his favourite chair.

Barry Gray, Hamilton Spectator.

March the priest sees the memoriam to Trisha in the newspaper and can barely look at the photo of the woman who was so beautiful and gentle, who had such strong faith.

Father Cote had stood in the church back then, trying to make sense of it, offer hope. It was one of the most difficult homilies he had ever spoken. There was no logic to why someone would do something like this, he told the congregation. Focus on faith and what still might come out of Trisha's death — in man's court, or God's. He referenced a short story by Tolstoy. The story was called "God Sees the Truth, but Waits."

Hamilton Police list the "Patricia Paraszczuk Homicide" on its "Help us solve these crimes" website link. Ray still hopes that one day a police officer will come knock on his door and bring him news of an arrest. Ray and Cathy will publish Trisha's obituary in the Hamilton Spectator *in March 2013, for the thirtieth straight year. Ray keeps a copy of the original "Eternal Pain" story that appeared in the* Spectator *handy and frequently reads it. Most of all he likes looking at the wedding picture of Trisha that ran in the paper. "She looks so life-like," he says.*

Part IV

Deadly Encounter

1

ANYBODY

Friday, January 14, 2005
O'Grady's Roadhouse
Upper James Street, Hamilton, Ontario

Friday night, good friends, hot wings, cold draught, and their song playing — Brenda and Art's. Brenda swayed under the lights on the tiny dance floor in her slim jeans, heels, scoop-necked white shirt. They used to sing karaoke to it together years ago while enjoying a few beers.

It was Janis Joplin singing "Me and Bobby McGee," a song about a couple hitching south, nothing in their future but a song and an unknown destination. Joplin's leathery voice, and the folksy 1960s rhythms carrying Brenda away once again.

> But feeling good was easy Lord, when he sang the blues
> Hey, feeling good was good enough for me
> Good enough for me and my Bobby McGee

Art? Her husband was close by, yet too far away. Off the dance floor, through the dingy lighting of the bar, back, behind a closed door, in a cramped hallway outside the bathroom. It could be anybody back there, beaten to the floor. But it was not. It was Art.

O'Grady's roadhouse, where Art Rozendal was beaten to death.

Another blow. Another. Art was defenceless; his only shield the mercy of his attackers — of which there was none. Blood was pooling in his eye sockets.

At the front of the bar, a customer rose from his table. He'd just got off work and needed to wash his hands. He walked to the back, opened the door to the hallway, and saw the man face down on the floor. His hand still gripping the doorknob, he stared at them, saw anger, cruelty, almost an evil light in the faces looming over the body.

"Do you want some of this?" one of them threatened.

A metallic flash. There was something in his mouth, like wire, almost like fangs. And now, the man's open hand pressed in the customer's face, against the jaw bone, casually shoving his head against the wall as he passed by.

They got away, all of them, past the bar, dance floor, out the front door, emerging from the heat into the cold on Upper James Street.

Beep. Beep. Beep.

Maloney rolled over and smacked the alarm on his night table. Morning? He rolled out of bed, staggered to the washroom in the dark, then returned to the bedroom.

John Rennison, *Hamilton Spectator.*

Lead homicide detective Mike Maloney.

Beep. Beep. Beep.

"Would you turn your pager off?" his wife murmured.

He stared at the night table. The pager. Now his eyes focused on the clock. He had only been asleep an hour or so. Was it just him, or did they always wait to call until after he had settled into a deep sleep? Homicide Detective Mike Maloney grabbed the pager, padded downstairs in his boxers to the living room, fumbled for the light switch, grabbed a piece of paper, and picked up the phone. Who am I calling anyway? he wondered. Had to be Peter. Maloney dialed. Detective-Sergeant Peter Abi-Rashed, senior man in the major crime unit of Hamilton Police, answered.

"Hello, this is Mike," Maloney said.

"What are you doing?" Abi-Rashed asked.

"What do you mean what am I doing?"

"We got one," Abi-Rashed muttered in the fatigued tone Maloney knew all too well. "You want to pay off your mortgage early?"

"It's already paid."

"You coming in?"

"I'm up now."

Maloney marched back upstairs, showered and shaved. He was 45, had 27 years under his belt as a cop in Hamilton, the past few years in homicide branch, and as he looked in the mirror at the blue eyes and face that stared back at him, he could see the wear of those years. But he wasn't an old man yet; there was still a boyishness, too.

He plugged in the iron. Domestic chores were not Maloney's strong suit. Ironing was an exception. During the week he always ironed the next day's dress shirt the night before. But this was supposed to be a weekend off. He slipped on the pressed shirt and the rest of his suit — the uniform homicide detectives were expected to wear when on the clock. Technically, he didn't have to report, but Maloney was well versed in the culture among his fellow detectives downtown. You get the call, you report.

He enjoyed the work, but was starting to think about hanging it up, leaving homicide. Sexual deviants, brain dead killers, bloody crime scenes, and, worst of all, connecting with families of murder victims — there was no closure for them, ever. Maloney could not remember once leaving court and truly feeling pleased with the result. It took a toll. He loved working with the detectives — best group he had been with in his years on the force — but enough was enough.

This new case was about to test Maloney's view of his job even more. Every murder matters; it's always tragic when someone takes life from another. But the reality, known all too well by those working homicide in Hamilton, was that many victims were people who routinely danced with the devil, who embraced high-risk lifestyles, or became trapped and got burned. But the victim in this new case was not one of those people. Not even close. Could have been anybody. That was what really turned the stomach; that's what would make this one linger with Mike Maloney more than most.

Maloney got in his car and started his drive to Central Station from his home in Ancaster. He drove down the Mountain, savouring the calm, Hamilton lying below enveloped in black. The thought occurred to Maloney at times like this: it was a nice looking city — and yet, down there something very bad had happened to somebody. The next 15 hours were going to be hell.

"Assault, 5-9-2 Upper James Street." The uniformed officer heard the call in his cruiser. A fight at a bar on a Friday night in Hamilton? Constable Ian Gouthro was hardly surprised. He had reported to his share of them. He was on patrol less than five minutes from the scene, which was a strip mall pub named O'Grady's Roadhouse. He radioed dispatch and said he would head over. Gouthro parked, walked to the front door. He expected to find a man inside with a bloody nose, the result of a routine liquor-induced scrap. By the time he marched inside O'Grady's, the latest information from dispatch indicated the suspects in the assault had fled. But entering a crowded and well-oiled bar after a fight was never a predictable situation.

"I've arrived," he said into his radio. "Entering."

"Do something! You gotta do something! He's in the back!"

Chaos, yelling, screaming. Gouthro's eyes adjusted to what seemed like an unusually dark bar. "Show me where he's at," he said, staring ahead.

All around were indistinguishable voices. He ignored them, ignored the milling throng; he had tunnel vision focused on the back of the building. Someone held open a door revealing the hallway by the bathroom. He noted a man on his back on the floor, blood on his nose and mouth, and a female on her knees beside him in hysterics.

"Do something, please! It's my husband. He's not breathing."

"Speed up the ambulance," he said into his radio.

Gouthro's heart pounded, but he kept his expression flat. He needed the woman's help until the paramedics arrived. He had a forceful but soft-spoken way about him.

"Look into my eyes," he said. "We're going to do this; we're going to get through this. Okay?"

She listened, nodded, did what she was told. She told the officer her name: Brenda Rozendal. Her husband's name was Art. Both were 44 years old. They had been married 20 years. Had two boys.

At that moment, in the white space between life and death, could Art sense anything? Did his mind's eye take him back through the past? The boy at home outside Hamilton, God's country, an infinite quilt of farmers' fields under a big sky; the young man with a thick moustache and broad smile hanging with his friend Bill in a garage, oil-stained hand clutching a silver wrench, lovingly bringing a classic car back to life — FM rock on the radio, and a cold OV waiting in the fridge; the grown man looking into Brenda's eyes at the kitchen table, the diamond sliding on to her finger, her nails shiny from a fresh coat of red polish.

The police officer and Brenda performed CPR. Brenda blew air into his lungs. There was no response. She could taste Art's blood on her tongue.

2

A SILVER FLASH

"Suspects are two black males. One: six foot, slim build, silver braces in mouth, bandana. Two: black jean jacket with a photo on the bottom right portion of the jacket."

It was 11:24 p.m. In his unmarked car, plainclothes constable Shane Groombridge held the wheel with his left hand and with his right scribbled the information relayed by dispatch in his notebook on the seat as he drove along Concession Street. Details of the suspects pretty vague, he thought — except for the silver braces. He had listened to the initial radio chatter about an assault at O'Grady's Roadhouse. He heard urgency in the voice of the officer on scene. *Speed up the ambulance.*

"Hotel three-five-two responding," Groombridge said into his radio. "Heading to the area to look for suspects."

That night Groombridge was working a night shift with the HEAT unit. High Enforcement Action Team officers investigate property crimes, stolen cars, gangs — whatever might be plaguing the community. Before heading out he reported to the station, attached the loaded Glock to his belt holster, put on a winter jacket, and checked out a Grand Am.

He parked his car on the police perimeter at the northeast corner of Brantdale Avenue, where it comes to a T-intersection at West 5th, and turned off the engine. He reclined in his seat to make himself even less visible through the tinted windows. About an hour had elapsed since the initial assault call. Too much time had passed, he thought. No way would the suspects still be hanging around in plain view inside the perimeter.

That's when he saw somebody emerge from the shadows, walking south across West 5th not far from his car, toward a house on the corner — male, at least six feet tall, dark clothing. Just before the man got to the door, he turned and walked west, across the lawn, back across West 5th. Made no sense. Why turn back? He walked toward the Hamilton Psychiatric Hospital grounds, across the parking lot and onto the snow-covered property. Groombridge started the car, eased it forward, and glided into the parking lot. The man was still walking with his back to him.

"Hotel three-five-two. Possible person of interest," he said into his radio. "Can you send some backup to give me a hand?"

According to the book, an officer does not approach a potentially violent suspect alone. You wait for backup. You never knew if the suspect had a weapon, or what his fighting skills might be, or if he was hopped up on something. But the man was getting closer to the rear of the HPH property. In seconds he would exit into the darkness, perhaps head down the Mountain.

Groombridge did not hesitate. He turned the ignition off, got out of the car, and moved across the lawn, snow crunching under his feet. He carried his radio and a notebook in his hand. The Glock sat ready in the belt holster. The firearm did not have a safety clip; it allowed for immediate firing.

"Hey, come here," Groombridge called. The man turned and faced him, saying nothing. Groombridge slipped his radio into his back pocket, unclipped his badge from his belt to show the suspect.

"What the fuck do you want?" the man demanded.

A silver flash. Didn't look like braces though, more like some kind of metallic mouthpiece. *This is the guy*, Groombridge thought. And the suspect was clearly agitated. Groombridge had to try to stall him until backup arrived.

"What's your name?" Groombridge asked.

"I don't have to fucking talk to you."

"There's been an assault at O'Grady's. You match the description of one of the suspects. Where are you coming from?"

The man swore again. "Am I under arrest? Am I under arrest?"

This was it. Groombridge knew from experience that when someone said words like that they were poised to bolt. And this guy's body language resembled a loaded spring. In a blur the cop's right hand grabbed the ball of the man's left shoulder.

"You're under arrest for assault."

Groombridge was not big for a police officer. At five foot ten, he was shorter than the suspect. But he had thick forearms and strong hands, and the swiftness of the move would have caught anyone by surprise, the hand digging into tissue and muscle like a vice. For someone who has never been in a fight, Groombridge's grip would have been the hardest hold he would have ever experienced. But the guy Groombridge grabbed was not going to submit. He pushed back and they locked arms. It was on.

They grappled for several metres. Groombridge had to stop the suspect from hitting him or fleeing, or, worst of all, grabbing his gun. He took him down, hard, pinning him to the ground, but the guy was strong; with adrenalin firing, he was still trying to kick and punch. Groombridge's bare hands pressed into the ice and snow, holding the arms with all his might. He heard a cruiser pull into the parking lot. Backup. It was a uniform, Ben Adams. Adams ran to the fight and pinned one of the arms. The suspect continued yelling, swearing, struggling. They cuffed him.

"Thanks, Ben," Groombridge said, breathing hard.

He read the man his rights, from memory, since the printout had flown with his notepad into the snow during the fight. He radioed dispatch. "Hotel three-five-two. Suspect under arrest." They searched him; placed the items in a bag: seventy dollars in cash, cigarettes, toothbrush, pick comb. Health card. His name was Kyro Sparks.

The baby was born on July 30, 1982, in Scarborough, a suburb of Toronto. The mother named her boy after Cairo, the Egyptian capital, which in Arabic means *victorious.*

Kyro Sparks had one memory of his biological father. He was maybe five or six. Kyro was with his mom, leaving a corner store. It was sunny. He felt really happy that day. Mom stopped to talk to some guy. Kyro looked up at this man he had never seen before.

"Say hi to your dad," Mom said. "That's your father."

And that was it. Not a sad memory or a happy one. Just … something, Kyro reflected. It was okay. Never bothered him or anything like that. Funny the things you remember. As for his stepfather, he wasn't abusive or anything. Kyro thought he was an asshole. It was kind of complicated.

As far as growing up, Kyro preferred to remember that he was the kid who always had the latest brand of Reebok, the new BMX bike, the white jumpsuit. Mom, she was like this angel, this glowing light that floated down upon him, put a toy in his hand, a Transformer, whatever, then hugs and kisses, and she was off to work. Mom and the stepfather worked for the post office. His stepfather gave him 50 bucks allowance. Let him hang at the park, too. On Sundays he could either go to church with his mom, or just hang at the park; his stepfather insisted on giving him the choice. Kyro got in some fights. Yeah, he got jumped a couple of times. Because he was a loudmouth. Sticking up for his brother, friends. Boys will be boys, he figured.

They lived near Markham Road and Lawrence Avenue. Kyro lived in the hood, yes, but it wasn't all that. That is, looking back, yes, it was the projects, but he was more like a hood star. What was a hood star? That's when things are bad but you act and talk like it's not bad. *A hood star.*

Kyro thought his first contact with police was kind of funny. He was making crank phone calls all the time, and one day the police come to the house.

"You Kyro Sparks? You making crank calls? You could go to jail for that."

His mom had put the cops up to it, he found out, trying to teach him a lesson. When he was about nine, his mom left the stepfather and they moved to Montreal. His mom then worked two or three jobs. She seemed sad all the time. Kyro was sleeping on the floor instead of in a bunk bed like he had in Toronto. They lived in a rough area of Montreal's South Shore, but this time Kyro didn't feel like a hood star. He didn't know why things weren't like they used to be. He wasn't getting the shoes and bikes anymore. Still wanted them, though.

It started small: the crime. Go to a variety store with a group of guys. Couple of them felt like a bag of chips, so they took the chips. They didn't have weapons, not all the time, although weapons were always around. What was one variety store guy going to do? You just ate the chips, looked right at the guy behind the counter. Said nothing; dared him to risk it over a bag of chips. There was beer sold in those variety stores, too. Cracked a few.

It didn't take long for Kyro to start wondering how much money the customer coming in the store had in his wallet. Understand? It wasn't as though, as a kid, Kyro said, "I want to be a felon." No, it was more like, "I want to get some money; in order to get it, I can do this." Funny, he never really planned on becoming what he did. Just kind of happened.

3

MORE THAN A FEELING

Saturday, January 15, 2005
Central Station, Major Crime Section
Hamilton, Ontario
1:30 a.m.

At his desk Detective Mike Maloney wrote the first bits of detail in a fresh white homicide notebook. Victim: Rozendal, Arthur 61/02/25. Suspect: Sparks, Kyro Jarreau James 82/07/30.

He noted the killing had occurred at O'Grady's Roadhouse. Small world. Back in 1977, when he was finishing high school at St. Thomas More, the bar was called Italian Village. It was just a few blocks from his school; the boys managed to get served there on occasion. Some of Art Rozendal's friends, he would learn, were people he had gone to school with.

Maloney grew up in the Mohawk Road and Garth Street area. His dad had worked at Dofasco; his mom stayed at home, but later worked at a fashion shop in Jackson Square. Maloney played Junior B hockey; some of his teammates were police officers. After graduating he figured it was either the fire department, the police, or teaching. He wrote the test to join the police service and started on May 14, 1977, in the cadet program. Over the years Maloney had worked a variety of posts, including the emergency response unit in the 1980s, where he did his share of busting through doors and windows. Good times, but he transferred out of ERU when it started to seem like every situation he entered involved a gun — including a close encounter with a round from a .357 Magnum.

Maloney had a suspect in the Rozendal case downstairs in lock-up, but first he left his desk and headed to the department's quiet room to meet the widow. He had been told Brenda Rozendal had seen her husband die at O'Grady's. He need to go slow, develop a rapport, he reminded himself.

Mike Maloney seemed to have the perfect personality to work homicide. Easygoing, nothing rattled him. What most didn't see was what brewed inside. When he met with the family of a murder victim, it got to him. How could he not feel their pain? Sometimes he wondered if he was more sensitive to these people than his own family. He tried to flip the switch, let it slide off him, but it never completely did.

He sat down with Brenda.

"I am so sorry for your loss," Maloney said. "I know there are places you'd rather be; people you'd rather be with."

He explained it was part of the process; he had to ask her what happened. It's one of the toughest parts of the job, asking a loved one to relive the experience. He listened to her account. The big question was: What had happened between Mr. Rozendal and his attackers at O'Grady's? Had there been some kind of provocation? Was Art capable of it? Maloney needed to learn more about Arthur Rozendal.

The boy crossed the street carrying his clothes in a garbage bag slung over his shoulder like a hobo. It was 1973 and Art was 12 years old. He walked toward the waiting car from the townhouse on Wendover Drive, just off Mohawk Road on the west Mountain in Hamilton. Art was about to meet his new family for the first time.

Arthur was born in Hagersville, south of Hamilton, on Saturday, February 25, 1961, the first child, and only son, of Cornelius (Neil) and Frances Rozendal. Neil and Frances would eventually also have two daughters: Debbie and Sandra. Art grew up in a rented house off Highway 6, beside Sumdrim Golf Club, just outside Caledonia. He attended nearby Oneida Public, a country school surrounded by farmers' fields.

In Grade 1 he met a boy named Bill Murray. They both played baseball; it was big in Oneida Township. Art played catcher; Bill pitched a bit, played a little first base. Their real connection, though, was cars — toy cars at first, but before long, real ones. Art was always drawing pictures of them, caricatures. He loved to draw, was good at it, too — a creative boy. He developed a love for a certain kind of car — 1960s and early 1970s Buicks, the Skylark and Gran Sport — perhaps drawn to the power and escapism the muscle car styling seemed to represent.

Art and Bill hung out a lot at the Murray farm, nestled among expansive rolling hills and pastures. The boys tooled away on an old beater that sat in a field. Probably seemed to their parents like they were just fooling around, but they were actually teaching themselves about how cars worked. One day, they were maybe nine or 10, they spent endless hours tooling around with an old dark blue 1962 Valiant wagon. It was an ugly car — all glass, a real fishbowl of a car. It had belonged to Bill's mom, but it had quit on her, and now it just sat in the field.

They actually got the engine to turn over. Art's eyes lit up.

"Let's do it."

Art jumped behind the wheel. Bill rode shotgun. There they were, booting around the field, laughing, triumphant, having brought the beast to life. The joyride didn't last long, mind you. Mrs. Murray was out the door, hollering at them to stop, thinking they'd kill themselves.

Fast-forward a couple of years; the Rozendals had moved from the country into Hamilton. But Art's family was breaking up. Neil worked as a long-haul truck driver, made runs up to Algoma Steel in Sault Ste. Marie. He had met a woman named Esther up there. They wanted to get married. Art's two sisters stayed behind with their mother in Hamilton, but Art decided to go with his dad, start a new life out west, in Winnipeg. It was difficult for Art to leave. But he had an adventurous spirit and loved his dad, though he was not always an easy man — old-school guy, taciturn, a disciplinarian.

And so Art carried his garbage bag of clothes to the car that day. Inside, waiting in the back seat, was a five-year-old boy named Darren and his baby sister, Cheryl. In the front was their mother, Esther, and the man who was about to become Esther's children's new stepdad, Neil Rozendal.

Neil had driven Esther and her children seven hours to Hamilton from Iron Bridge, a town up near Sudbury. Darren didn't understand everything that was going on, but knew he was in for a long ride, and it was just beginning. His parents had broken up; his mom was now with Neil, who was taking the newly blended family out to Winnipeg. And he knew he was getting a new brother.

Art loaded his clothes in the trunk of the car, and Neil drove the family up north for a stop in Iron Bridge, then on to Winnipeg. Darren slept nestled in the footwell of the car like a kitten. Art Rozendal now had a stepbrother and stepsister — although he would never use those words. From the start Darren and Cheryl were simply his brother and sister. Period. Art's heart was too big to ever allow him to feel they were anything but part of him.

His new family made the trip in his new stepmother's car: an orange Buick. Everything had instantly changed. At least the uncertain road ahead would be travelled in a 1967 Skylark.

At Art's suggestion his dad applied for a job managing a big hog farm near Winnipeg. In 1974 he landed the position, which came with a large but run-down house on the property, where the family settled. Everyone pitched in to fix up the place. Art worked hard on the farm, loaded feed mixed with water that was piped into a series of pig barns, shovelled manure. He developed an allergic reaction to pig hair; it made his skin flake, and his hands would sometimes crack and bleed. Kids at school teased him. It didn't help that when you work on a pig farm, the smell stayed with you.

"I can smell Art coming now," the kids would say.

He rolled with it, laughed it off.

Art had moved a couple of thousand kilometres from home, left his mother and sisters behind in Hamilton, and now worked hard, labouring when not in school — at a job that caused others to mock him. He had plenty of fodder for bitterness, but Art's genial manner did not change from the carefree days in the Caledonia countryside.

Art was no saint; he got in hot water with a buddy when they were caught with beer at a sleepover after a high-school dance. He cursed when things went bad, would toss in a four-letter word here and there, especially when he tooled away on a car in the garage. But no one ever saw him get truly angry. Art had more patience than most, and could fit in with most situations, was good at talking to people.

Cars continued to be his first love through high school. He'd always been creative, and faded muscle cars in need of restoration became his canvas. Shiny new chrome, hot paint job, an engine resurrected to its former growl — cars took Art wherever he needed to go. He socked away cash working on the farm and bought Esther's 1967 Skylark, fixed it, and painted it a rust colour.

He worked on other cars with his friends, Paul Willems and Dave Newman. All three lived on farms within a few kilometres of one another, near a town called Dugald. When they went out, Art always drove — to a party, the roller rink, hanging at Juniors Restaurant in downtown Winnipeg. They cruised Portage Avenue on a Sunday summer's night — a Winnipeg tradition — alongside other souped-up hot rods on display, on occasion opening up the Skylark for an impromptu drag race.

Art's new brother, Darren, came to see him as both a father figure and big brother. Darren never did see eye-to-eye with his stepdad, Neil. He came to wonder if he was perhaps baggage in Neil's life. For Art's dad there was a right and wrong way to do everything, whether it was table manners or anything else. Art got into arguments with his dad, too, but it never seemed to get too intense. It was different with Darren, who had a more rebellious spirit.

Art always let Darren hang at the garage at Paul's place when they worked on a car. He invited Darren and sister, Cheryl, along when he drove into town — not because his parents told him to, but because he wanted to. He took them to see movies — *Star Wars*, *The Jungle Book*. In 1978 Art and Paul snuck Darren into *American Hot Wax*, a 1950s nostalgia flick. He took them to Grand Beach on Lake Winnipeg, 70 kilometres north of the city, billed as one of the best inland beaches in the world. They swam, threw the Frisbee and football around with Art's buddies. Years later Darren wondered why on earth Art had let his little brother and sister hang with him. But Darren loved every minute of it. Art was cool, smart, and responsible. He was all that.

Around 1980 the family left the hog farm and moved into Winnipeg; Neil had suffered a heart attack and got a new job at a city feed mill. Art went to high school in the day, worked at night at a fish processing plant, saving his money for a car and a trip east he had long been planning. Art and Darren had their own rooms on the farm, but in the city they now shared bunk beds. That meant Darren grew up listening to Art's music. His big brother owned a stereo, a lumbering wooden console where the lid opened to reveal the radio and turntable. Art played classic rock: Eagles, Elton John, Triumph. He spun the Boston hit "More Than a Feeling" all the time:

> It's more than a feeling, when I hear that old song they
> used to play
> I begin dreaming
> Till I see Marianne walking away

As soon as Art graduated high school, he said he was heading back east to Ontario. When Darren heard Art was leaving, he was heartbroken; he'd had no inkling that Art wanted to return to Hamilton, or that he was leaving for good. Art hadn't even finished the 1970 Buick GSX he had been refurbishing at Paul's garage. He never talked much about his reasons for going. Darren was bitter, but not with his brother. He believed he may have left in part because Art wasn't getting along with Neil. Art's stepmother, Esther, believed he just wanted to start fresh, wanted to find a job in southern Ontario. Neil said nothing to try to stop Art from doing what he felt was best, and he was of a generation that did not tend to emote. He loved his son and it hurt to see him go, but he was also not the type to express those feelings. After Art left, Darren's arguments with his stepfather grew worse. He started to rebel, skipping school. What was going to happen to Darren with Art gone?

4

CUT AND RUN

Saturday, January 15, 2005
Central Station Lockup
1:00 a.m.

Hamilton forensic detective Annette Huys observed the suspect through the window in the cell door. Kyro Sparks had followed directions to remove his footwear — a pair of Timberland hiking-style boots, she noted — and belt, as well as a hooded sweater. Huys noticed what looked like blood on the Timberlands.

She confirmed the hunch later, applying a Hemastix strip to the boots to test for blood. The result came up positive — whose blood it was was another question, though. Huys (pronounced *Huze*) opened the cell door, introduced herself. Kyro Sparks was wearing socks, a shirt, and baggy blue pants. She said they needed him to remove his clothes. He would be issued a jumpsuit to wear.

"You're not getting anything," he said.

Huys asked again.

"Fuck you, bitch," he replied, and moved toward her. She closed the cell door.

"We can do this the easy way or the hard way," she said through the door.

She was tired and didn't need this. The evening had been a long one for Huys. She had met senior ident man Gary Zwicker at Hamilton General Hospital earlier that evening. After getting called to work the

O'Grady's homicide, they reported to the ER. On a bed in the trauma suite, they had viewed the body and taken photos. Then, they had bagged the victim's hands to preserve potential forensic evidence — perhaps he scratched one of the killers in the struggle, had skin or blood under his nails — gently tying sterile paper bags around each hand with string to protect them. After returning to Central Station, Huys had stored the victim's clothes in an evidence locker and headed to the holding cells. There she met with Shane Groombridge and other officers outside Kyro Sparks's cell.

She again asked Kyro Sparks for his clothes. He refused again. This was not going to go well. He was over six feet tall, and Huys, who was five foot four, was taken aback by his anger. The metal grills on his teeth added to his intimidating appearance.

"You can't do anything to me. Why don't you Tase me?" Sparks said. "Go ahead, bitch."

"I don't think I'd want to be getting Tasered with all that metal in your mouth," Huys said through the closed window on the door.

She'd never met a suspect so combative. There had been a suspect who, just before Huys had photographed his hands, had punched a wall with each fist, as though trying to destroy his knuckles and alter forensic evidence. Crazy. But Sparks was off the charts.

Huys had started with Hamilton police in 1997. Before that she had worked for the Ontario Provincial Police as a civilian monitor of wire taps in intelligence investigations. Odd hours, shift work, and there were times she had to listen to everything going on in a household. Such an invasion of privacy, hearing them with their partners — everything. She had heard many things that she never wanted to hear, but that was the job. She started with ident in January 2003, the department's first female detective. They teased her; she was tagged "forensic Barbie" and given a toy doll. She played right along, kept the Barbie doll in the locker given to her, accessorized with a lab coat and gun belt.

Kyro Sparks continued shouting through the cell, spitting on the door. Huys told Groombridge she needed help to get the clothes. Groombridge, along with several others, including officer Ben Adams, opened the door and walked in.

"We need your clothes for evidence," Groombridge said.

"Fuck you. Are you going to Tase me? Go ahead. Tase me. I've been shot, survived a bullet to the head; I can survive this. You're going to have to take them from me."

They left the cell. Minutes later, an officer arrived with a Taser, a rod that sends a type of electrical shock called a dry stun. Sparks pointed at a line on the floor marking the threshold separating the cell from the hallway.

"I bet if I cross that line you'll Tase me."

The officer tried to calm him down again. Sparks continued moving toward the line and the open door.

He was almost out the door when five officers wrestled him to the ground. He kept struggling; his strength was impressive. The Taser was applied, and with the electricity rippling through his nervous system, the silver grills popped out of his mouth and clinked onto the jail floor. Blood became visible in his mouth; perhaps it had been cut by the mouthpiece.

Tasering is painful; it is used to temporarily immobilize the muscles of someone. It worked on Sparks, or so it seemed. Thinking that Sparks had been immobilized, the officers started removing his clothes. Remarkably, he resumed the fight. It is rare for a suspect to continue to fight after being Tasered. He was shocked again, and his body went limp. The clothes were finally removed, revealing the fact that Kyro Sparks wore long underwear from the waist down.

At 3:30 a.m. Detective Mike Maloney finished his first interview with Brenda Rozendal. It had lasted an hour. He asked her about Art, his personality, and whether anyone would want to hurt him. There was another person sitting in on the interview as well. He was required to be there, because, in fact, he had been at O'Grady's Roadhouse, too. It was Art's eldest son, Neil. Maloney asked him about what he had seen at O'Grady's.

Maloney left the quiet room to meet with Kyro Sparks downstairs. He had news for his suspect. The initial charge had been assault. Maloney now wanted to tell him that he might well be charged with murder. But before he made it down to the cells, Maloney received an update: Kyro Sparks had been combative in his cell. He had been Tasered. Maloney's mouth dropped. Tasered? *Now I'll never get a statement from the guy,* he thought. And even if Sparks did talk, how would it ever stand up in court? Maloney headed for the lockup, fuming. He knew the uniform guys had a job to do, and that Sparks had been out of control, but in a homicide investigation it was crucial to always be mindful that anything said or done might be used in court. He could all but hear the judge now: "Yes, Mr. Sparks, did the officers treat you properly, fairly in custody? And you gave this statement of your own free will?"

At the cell an officer checked on Sparks.

"What, punk-ass?" Sparks barked at the uniform, and spat at the door. He had managed to move his cuffed hands from behind his back to his front by stepping through the loop. He was doing push-ups on the floor.

Maloney arrived outside the closed cell door along with Detective Peter Abi-Rashed. Maloney was the lead investigator in the case; Abi-Rashed, the case manager.

"Do you want to talk?" Abi-Rashed said through the closed window of the cell.

"About what?" Kyro Sparks replied.

Maloney opened the cell door and entered. "My name is Detective Mike Maloney. I need to tell you about your change in jeopardy. You were brought in for assault. It is now murder."

"What murder?"

"The guy you assaulted."

"What guy, what murder — this is bullshit."

"The guy you assaulted died."

"What guy? I don't know about no guy and no murder."

Maloney left and retrieved a phone for Kyro Sparks to speak to a legal aid lawyer in private. He returned at 5:00 a.m.

"My lawyer told me not to say anything," Sparks said.

"You don't have to say anything," Maloney replied.

"I've been treated like an animal here."

"I've been told that apparently you acted inappropriately earlier. What were you doing in the neighbourhood where you were arrested?"

"Give me a cigarette and I'll tell you where I was from morning 'til night."

"We don't have any cigarettes. Where did the blood on your shoes come from?"

"It's my blood. From two or three months ago. Can't get it out."

Maloney asked if he would come to a room to talk on video. "Or would you rather go back to the cells?"

"What do you think?"

"Do you want to speak on video?"

"No way."

At 8:00 a.m. Maloney drove home. His wife and kids were still asleep. With some cases Maloney would crack a lite beer after a long shift, sit back, and unwind before turning in. But with this one, he knew, as the primary investigator, he'd be going right back to the office, so it was straight to bed. Four hours later he was back on the case, organizing a photo lineup with Kyro Sparks in it.

That evening Maloney drove up the Mountain for his first look at the crime scene. Annette Huys and Gary Zwicker were processing the area inside O'Grady's. They gave Maloney a walk-through of where Art Rozendal had died. Maloney had no idea that, just a couple of blocks away, the second of the killers was making a run for it

On Saturday afternoon Kyro Sparks was still sitting in his cell downtown; at the same time, Cory McLeod was in an apartment just a couple of blocks up the street from O'Grady's Roadhouse. All day Cory had tried to track down Kyro. No answer on his cell phone. Didn't make sense. Where could he be? They were both from out of town: Kitchener. Kyro had a cousin in Hamilton, but the cousin hadn't seen him. Kyro's girlfriend, Katrina McLennan, a student at Mohawk College in Hamilton, didn't know where he was, either.

Cory sat in Katrina's apartment. Her friend, Sherri Foreman, was Cory's girlfriend, and often stayed in the same apartment. Nobody had seen Kyro since the night before, Friday, when all four of them had been in the apartment moments after the incident at O'Grady's. Cory had urged Kyro not to leave the apartment. Cops would be looking for them everywhere. Kyro was angry, though. He and Cory had been arguing over stuff all night, so he took off.

Saturday afternoon the local dinner hour news came on TV. The lead story was about a murder. It showed a picture of O'Grady's. Cory's attention perked up. A mug shot photo flashed on the screen. It was Kyro. Cory felt his mind spin. The TV reporter said Hamilton police had one man in custody: Kyro Jarreau Sparks, 23, of Kitchener. Police were looking for at least one other man in connection with the murder.

The victim's name was Arthur Rozendal. Cory watched the video cut to the home of the victim; a teenage boy crying. It was one of Arthur Rozendal's sons: Jordan, 15. The boy was on TV, in tears, asking why someone would do this to his dad.

Cory stared at the screen. Someone? Him. It was him. Kyro and Cory had beaten on that guy in the bar. The guy had never even got a punch in, Cory reflected.

Cory decided that he wasn't sticking around any longer. He was on his feet, out the door, and entered a convenience store close by, one he'd often used while staying at the apartment. He picked up the payphone and called a cab. He'd just got off the phone when someone walked in, a man dressed in business clothes. Looked like an official visit. A cop? The guy started putting questions to the guy behind the counter. He had to be a plainclothes cop.

So, Cory was thinking: okay, he's asking about us. Cory had been in the store many times, for food, or picking up Century Sams — a type of cigar he used to roll joints. Now, here was this cop asking this Chinaman behind the counter if he'd seen any black faces in there. *And I'm right here*, Cory thought. His mind raced. He was getting ready to cut and run. *No*, he thought. *Stay put. Wait.* The cop finished talking to the guy behind the counter and left. Too close. Minutes later, the cab pulled out front, took Cory downtown to the bus station.

On the Greyhound back to Kitchener, Cory McLeod kept replaying the night. Okay. They'd had some drinks. Played some pool. Then the fight. What did the cops have? What had he left behind? His drinking glass on the table? He felt for his neck chain, the one that had dog tags attached. *They have my fucking chain.* At least his name wasn't on the dog tags, or even his initials. The inscription was just his nickname: Daymein P. Even if they found something, DNA somewhere, he figured that it would take a long time to come up with his name, find him, and arrest him. The plan: Take care of business in Kitchener and leave the country. By the time they came looking for him, he would be gone.

5

INTERSECTION

Cory McLeod's relatives were originally from Jamaica, a place where, Cory had heard, several members of his extended family did time in jail — for what, he wasn't sure. He was born in 1985, and knew his biological father, although he didn't remember him being around much. As Cory reached his teens, they had built more of a rapport. His father worked as a Waterloo police officer, and later was a school board trustee in Kitchener. He lived at his grandmother's; in fact a lot of his family stayed in the house.

His mother, Kathy, wanted to make a better life for her kids. She joined the Canadian military and moved the family to Halifax when he was nine, after she had separated from Cory's stepfather. In Halifax Cory got into drug dealing and stealing with his friends. One day he robbed an older man, who was a dealer. The guy was well respected —feared, really — in the community. After the robbery the guy sent a pack of guys after Cory; they messed him up pretty good, beat on him with steel pipes. He ended up in the hospital for a week.

When he was 13, Cory moved back to Kitchener by himself, lived with an aunt. He attended St. Anne's elementary school. Didn't last long, though. The school was almost all white; the only black kids were Cory and a few of his cousins. A lot of the kids were from wealthy families, from good neighbourhoods, and he and his cousins were from downtown, broke.

One day Cory saw a white kid picking on his cousin in the school hallway. His cousin was a yappy kid, in Grade 4; Cory was in Grade 7. All

Cory saw was this bigger white kid, in Grade 8, picking on his little cousin. Was the guy calling his cousin a nigger? Spitting on him? Cory lost it, fought the kid. Cory was not a big boy, and the Grade 8 kid got in some punches.

Cory's hat fell off in the fight. A teacher picked it up and took it away. He was sent to the office, and then, later, Cory went to the teacher's office to retrieve his hat. He was still burning.

"I want my hat back."

"Say please," he heard the teacher reply.

Cory got angrier; the teacher told Cory to just leave, and placed his hand on Cory's shoulder. Cory snapped. He started screaming and hit the teacher in the face, over and over. A janitor jumped in to break it up. Cory got kicked out of school. Why did it bother him so much to have the teacher put his hand on him? He didn't think he was obsessive about it. If a friend touched him, it was fine, but if a man put his hand on him in an aggressive manner, that was not only an insult, it was a threat. And if a man threatened him, he was going to defend himself.

Cory was suspended for four days; later he was kicked out of the school. They couldn't expel him since he was under 16, but they basically said, "Don't enroll again and we won't charge you."

He went back to Halifax. Then back to Kitchener. Back and forth. His mom moved back to Kitchener to be closer to him. He enrolled at Cameron Heights high school. Lasted about two weeks there. Was getting heavier into drugs, crime, living here and there. Got into crack; hung with a friend who stole car stereos, which they sold to drug dealers in Kitchener. Was convicted under the Young Offender's Act for robbery.

One day, when he was about 15, he met a guy in Kitchener named Kyro Sparks through one of his uncles, Kyro was a year older, but they clicked; had similar backgrounds. Kyro had moved to Kitchener from Montreal when he was 16. A radical change from a crummy apartment in Montreal to living with an aunt who seemed to him well off, lived in the Doon Valley area, had a pool with a diving board. He missed some friends in Montreal, but how could anyone ever be upset about moving to a place like Kitchener, Kyro wondered.

His first day of high school at KCI, Kitchener Collegiate Institute, a staff member took Kyro Sparks aside. "I don't want any big city gangsters coming in here causing trouble," she told him.

So that's it, thought Kyro. *That's what I am? I am from the big city. Yeah, that's right.* Other students, they were giving him the same thing: "Yo, bro, are you a Crip or a Blood?" Kyro grinned at it all. Didn't think of himself as anything but a little snotty kid. But he started enjoying the attention, played it up. Started wearing different clothes than the others. Got in trouble. Around that time he started smoking a lot of marijuana. It was weird: in Montreal, guys bought drugs, did a bit, but sold most of it to make money. Here, the kids were rich. They bought it to get high, and that was it. Kids doing acid, smoking weed all day, skipping class every day. He was one of them.

In Kitchener he hung out with some friends who called one another by the nickname "King." You know, *King*: pride of the people. Black people, Kyro reflected, they've been convinced they are slaves of the world, but it wasn't so. In fact it was the exact opposite. So Kyro said, "What's up, King? Here is my Queen." That swagger came out in the rap music Kyro made. He even made a homemade album. He called it *Heaven Sent And Hell Raising.*

One day someone ripped off Kyro. Kyro and some friends took care of it. Went and got back what was his. There was a gun involved. In court they were saying that Kyro and the others were part of a gang called the Kings. Got 16 months for it, was put in the bucket in Cambridge, then Guelph, before being kicked out of there for carrying a concealed weapon in prison. Anything can happen in prison, right? *Gotta be prepared,* he thought. In jail he was getting more of the gangster thing, was grouped on ranges with guys from Toronto, gang members, black guys. "Yeah," people told him, "you're one of those Toronto guys."

His identity, cultivated as a boy in Montreal, reinforced in Kitchener, was now formalized in prison. Was he a badass? That's what he was told. And he was doin' it. Kyro was like, "Okay, it is what it is."

His friendship with Cory McLeod was interrupted by jail time. Cory was put on ice first, for armed robbery; he did time with his buddy Dwayne. They were 17. Dwayne got nine months; Cory, 15. Later, Cory was also charged in a stabbing attack. He proclaimed his innocence, was certain he'd be found not guilty in the end. Some guy ratted him out that hadn't even seen who attacked him; just threw Cory's name in there.

He decided he wasn't going to stick around to learn his fate. He hit the road, for Hamilton — a place to lie low for a while, out of sight of the Kitchener police, hang with his girlfriend, Sherri Foreman, and figure out his next move. Funny thing: in Hamilton, Cory ran into Dwayne, and the guy had become a born again Christian. No more drink, weed, sex. Totally committed his life to God. Sherri started calling him preacher boy.

"This man did all this shit with me, now he's found God?" Cory said.

He laughed at him. But they hung out. Dwayne wanted Cory to come to church with him. Think about getting baptized, turning it all around like he had. Cory was dubious, but went to church with him one day.

"I think there's someone in here who needs to be saved," said the minister.

Cory grinned.

"You set me up," he said to Dwayne.

"You gotta come get baptized," Dwayne told him.

"Right."

Cory thought about it, though. Might be something to consider. But he would put that off for a while.

In January 2005, Cory, 19, was still on the run in Hamilton. Kyro Sparks, 22, hung in the city, too. Kyro had worked through temp agencies on and off in Kitchener. Had his forklift licence. Maybe he could get a job in Steeltown, he figured.

They hung with their girlfriends, Katrina and Sherri, at an apartment on Upper James Street. Cory and Kyro started to frequent a bar just around the corner from the apartment. They'd get some food, play pool, drink some beer, double Crown Royals, Grand Marnier. The bar was called O'Grady's Roadhouse.

While his childhood buddy Art Rozendal had been living in Winnipeg, Bill Murray finished Grade 8 at Oneida Public then went on to Cayuga High School. As his senior year wound down, Dofasco came recruiting for their steel mills, and Bill got hired. On a summer day in 1980, a month or two after he started on the job, Bill came home from work to find Art in his driveway. He had come home. And in the driveway with

Art was an old Buick Gran Sport GSX. It was like they had never been apart; they picked up right where they left off, and the next night they're working on the Buick.

Art dreamed of being a veterinarian, and got accepted at the University of Guelph's acclaimed veterinary school. But money was an issue. To save he was living at his mom's place off Mohawk Road. He never did enroll at U of G. A more immediate way to earn a solid living was using his expertise with tools and machines. He wanted to get hired at Dofasco like his friend Bill, but there were no positions open. He was able to walk right into the job at Big Steel competitor Stelco, though. He worked as a millwright, or industrial mechanic — someone who maintains and repairs machinery. He was stationed in the coke ovens.

Whenever Art and Bill's shifts coincided, they spent time off working on cars at Bill's place. He had a big garage out in the country. They could fit half a dozen cars in there, put them up on blocks — old street rods, muscle cars. Art loved his Buicks and Bill was a Chrysler guy. They always checked newspapers for spare parts, went to car shows — part of a network of car guys in the area. Sometimes they fixed cars for resale; other times just did it for fun. Put the radio on, listen to some Zeppelin, and crack a few Old Vienna beers. Art had a special affinity for body work, chrome, paint. Given Art's roots, cars had long been his focus, but he could have just as easily have been a commercial artist, perhaps a sculptor. He had that kind of imagination and ability.

Art was Bill's best man at his wedding in 1982 — that same year he met a 22-year-old woman named Brenda Merrill. She was a year older than Art, had grown up in the Bruce Park neighbourhood on the Mountain. Brenda had hazel eyes, red-brown hair, and small features. She never believed in love at first sight, and did not love Art off the bat. But when they met, she instantly locked eyes — it was like she could stare right into his soul, feel his kindness, empathy. She knew from the start she would marry him someday.

Art fell hard for Brenda. He'd had girlfriends in Winnipeg, but nothing too serious. Brenda was different. She was funny, outgoing, said what was on her mind. He talked her up to his friends all the time, unabashedly telling them how amazing she was, how much he loved her. They never really talked marriage, but discussed buying a house together. In May 1983 they viewed a house on Carrick and knew it was the one. They put an offer in, even though neither of them had much money. Art had a solid job but spent most of his money on cars. He said he would sell his blue Trans Am.

They headed to Jackson Square for lunch. Afterward, Art went off on his own for a bit, shopping. Later, back up at Brenda's family home, hanging with Art, Brenda was thinking, I just bought a house with a man; we've never talked about marriage, and we're not engaged. What am I doing? She had just finished painting the last coat of red on her nails at the kitchen table, when Art pulled out the ring he had bought hours earlier and proposed. After teasing Art — "Couldn't you have at least proposed in the park or something?" — Brenda slipped on the diamond.

Brenda and Art wed on June 8, 1985, at New Westminster Presbyterian Church, the reception held at the old Glass Workers Hall down on Barton and Lottridge Streets. A couple of years later, they moved from their house on Carrick into the home that had belonged to Brenda's family. Art renovated and expanded the place, Brenda's mom lived downstairs in a basement apartment. Their first son was born May 20, 1986. Art named him after his father, Neil. Their second son, Jordan, was born September 3, 1989.

Two years later they went through a tough time. Brenda had two aneurysms, right around Art's 30th birthday. When she got out of the hospital, they decided to renew their vows, having a refreshed appreciation for their love and lives. Rev. John Hibbs, who had married them, did the honours.

Their son Neil was diagnosed with epilepsy in Grade 6. Neil was teased at school after he had a couple of seizures. A couple of kids called him "devil child"; it drove him to tears. But Neil thrived on love and laughter at home. His dad had a madcap sense of humour that Neil inherited. Art loved watching comedies with his kids; the animated movie *Ice Age* was a favourite, especially the squirrel in the quest for a single acorn that eluded him.

Back in Winnipeg, meanwhile, Art's brother, Darren, had hit tough times. He had a young son, but he and his girlfriend had just split up. She moved east to Mississauga and took the boy. Darren wanted to be closer to him. Although he felt some reservations about it, he phoned Art one day and asked if he could stay with him for a while until he got his own place.

Hamilton Spectator.

Art and Brenda with Neil and Jordan.

"When can you be here?" Art said without hesitation.

Darren had kept in touch with Art since he left Winnipeg, and knew how big his heart was, but this time even he was taken aback. Art was married, with kids, a house, and Darren hadn't seen him in a while. And yet Art had instantly invited his brother into his home? But that was Art.

Back in Hamilton Darren was again connected with his brother, and the huge family dinner gatherings at the Rozendal house that Art was famous for organizing. Art had extended family spread around southern Ontario, and of course there was his mom, and sisters Debbie and Sandi. His dad, Neil, had now settled up in Ironbridge in northern Ontario with his second wife, Esther, and Art often drove the boys up to visit.

At home for Thanksgiving, Art set tables together stretching the length of the living room and dining room, packing in 15, 20 people — family and friends, aunts, cousins. Art stood, formally thanking everyone for coming, said a prayer. He often cooked the food, too, famous for his double chocolate cheesecake, or his marinated barbecued steaks — both recipes he gleefully refused to share.

Christmas was legendary at the house. Art made a huge show of it. When Neil and Jordan were young, he would put a tiny pine cone in the Christmas tree holder, get them all around it and sang "O Christmas Tree." Then the kids would go to school. When they came back, the full tree would be up.

"Look!" Art would exclaim. "The singing paid off!"

Art doted on his boys as they grew, always surprised them with unusual present wrappings he created himself, and built each of them their own custom-made theme beds. For Christmas 2004, Art bought Jordan a chopper-style bicycle that was only available in the U.S., and a computer for Neil. He unveiled the gifts Christmas morning in the garage, wrapped in unique boxes that he'd created.

For Valentine's Day 2004, Art presented Brenda with a crown and dressed up in full knight's regalia as Sir Arthur. "Dear Lady," he wrote her. "Allow me to introduce myself. I am your knight for the day." He wrote messages on white cards, each accompanied by a gift:

> First, a fine love potion noted for its ability to start your day in the most delightful way, much as your smile does to mine. Second, a flower so fair but not as fair as thee. Third, treats for the taste buds that match your nature. Please note, they are also a bit nutty. Fourth, jewels to match the sparkle in your eyes. May you wear it always knowing you are my Queen. Fifth, words crafted by the

greatest artisans in the land to woo you, it being said
I sometimes don't say it often enough. And lastly, my
undying love and devotion. I hope to have you near me
always!
Happy Valentines,
A

One night, remembering that Brenda had once said that just once
she'd like to dance to music in the rain, Art put a speaker out on the porch,
pulled her out into a rain shower on the driveway and danced with her.

"Art," Bill Murray joked later, "you're making the rest of us look bad."

Art laughed. He was just being himself; didn't care how it looked to
others. Perhaps he had instinctively gone the opposite of his old-school
father, not just feeling love but openly expressing it.

And that went for his male friends, too. Art was a rugged-looking
country boy, with thick mustache who stood five foot nine and weighed
200 pounds — although Bill swore he was six feet — a gear-head, hard
hat-wearing fixer of heavy machinery, and yet he had the biggest and
softest heart around. Among his friends he was known for The Hug. He
would hug a buddy upon seeing him. It wasn't gushy, or phony, just a
sign of genuine affection. Other guys could feel that kind of emotion, but
hadn't the nerve to express it. Art put it out there, unafraid.

At work this ability allowed him to play the peacemaker on occasion.
He needed his friends to get along. On the job at Stelco, if he ever saw a
couple of the guys going at it, arguing, he would intervene. "C'mon, guys,
we don't need the fighting, we're brothers," he said.

Brenda and Art loved the Bruce Park neighbourhood where they
lived. It was tight-knit; everyone knew everyone else. One of the places
they had started to gather some evenings was a roadhouse a few blocks
away. It wasn't the fanciest place, just a wings and beer place in a strip
mall, but the location was perfect and the food was good. They could
walk there, with their sons, have a few beers, dance. Brenda would get a
burger, Art hot wings. They knew everyone there.

On Friday, January 14, 2005, Art had just got off a night shift and
returned home at 9:00 a.m. from Stelco. It was cause for a celebration of
sorts, the end to a series working evenings. He needed a rest, but first he

took Brenda to McMaster Hospital for a cardiac stress test. When they got back to the house in the afternoon, he had a nap. Bev, Brenda's sister, called the house around noon, checking up on Brenda. Art answered. Bev had just got back the week before from England; she had a girlfriend over there whose husband passed away suddenly on Christmas Eve, and she had gone over for the funeral. Art was very close with Bev and always liked talking with her. He wanted to know all about her trip, and how her grieving friend was doing.

"What are you two doing tonight?" Bev asked.

"Might go out. Why don't we get together tomorrow night?" Art said.

"Okay, let's do it."

"Talk to you later. Love you."

Saturday afternoon Art drove his youngest son, Jordan, to work at McDonald's. The plan was that Art, Brenda, and Neil would head out for dinner, and Jordan would join them after he got off work. At 6:30 p.m. the three of them left the house. It was a clear, cold night; the ground was snow-covered but the sidewalk bare. It took them maybe 10 minutes. They usually knew most everyone in the place. Tonight would be different. Their lives were about to intersect with a few young men they had never seen before. Art and his family walked in the door at O'Grady's Roadhouse on Upper James Street.

6

CRUEL COWARDICE

Art and Brenda greeted staff they knew well, like Cheryl, a waitress, and the bartender Michelle. They sat with Neil at their usual table. Art wore blue jeans, belt, checked blue shirt tucked in, white Nike running shoes, and work socks. Brenda wore heels, white shirt, jeans; Neil, jeans and black T-shirt. Art and Neil ordered hot wings, as usual. Brenda got fried mozzarella sticks and a salad. Art ordered a pitcher of Canadian draught.

The place started getting busier. After eating, Brenda chatted with friends; Art and Neil played pool at the tables. Stripes and solids. Art didn't go easy on his son, and Neil didn't want him to; he wanted to see if he could beat his dad. Art was a good player, chided Neil about it. "Oh, come on Neil, you could have made that shot … let me show you how it's done."

Cheryl brought Art a bottle of Export, then a Labatt 50.

There were two men playing at a table next to theirs. They had never seen them before. In the close quarters of the pool table area, the four of them on occasion took turns taking shots so as not to get in the way of the other, avoid accidentally poking one another with a pool cue. Etiquette. The two young men were Kyro Sparks and Cory McLeod.

Cory and Kyro finished their game, sat back at their own table, where they had ordered two pounds of wings and a pitcher of beer. The two of them kept jawing at each other, arguing. Nagging each other about their situations: the fact that Kyro couldn't find work in Hamilton and that Cory was on the run for an assault charge in Kitchener; the fact that neither was making any money so were staying at Katrina and Sherri's apartment around the corner. Both guys were stretched, throwing around cash they didn't have.

Brenda hit the dance floor with a girlfriend, just after 10:00 p.m. "Me and Bobby McGee" had just started playing. Brenda loved that song. Art was a good dancer and enjoyed it, but this time he walked past Brenda, did a mock jig with her, and then begged off. He wasn't up for more. He was tired, from work, and now the food, drinks.

A friend ordered another pitcher for Art and Brenda, which they had yet to start. Art was weary but in a great mood. Up at the bar, he chatted with a buddy named Randy, and Cheryl. Meanwhile, Neil said goodbye to his mom on the dance floor. He was heading home to meet Jordan and bring him back to O'Grady's. He stopped at the bar. Art was doing a shot of Forty Creek Whisky, his favourite.

"Going to get Jordan," Neil said. And he was out the door.

Brenda was still dancing; Art deciding that now — not earlier, and not later, but now — was the time to go to use the bathroom. He walked from the bar.

Cory was still going at it with Kyro, arguing, needling. Kyro was getting hot. Who was going to start making some cash? "How long can we expect the chicks to fucking put up with us?" Cory said. Tempers were rising. Cory was a hustler, always had been; talking is what he did. Kyro wasn't like that. He was angry.

In seconds Art reached the back of the bar, perhaps walking past Cory and Kyro's table, opened the door that separated the bar and dance floor area from a short, narrow back hallway. The door closed, he opened the bathroom door on his left, and entered.

Kyro had had enough of Cory. He got up from their table, walked to the back. There was just one urinal in the bathroom. Art was there using it. Kyro entered the small bathroom and stood behind Art. They were together.

Kyro told Art to hurry up, said he needed to use the urinal. Art turned, but there was barely space to maneuver. Genial as always, and having had several drinks, Art put his hand on Kyro's shoulder, and suggested Kyro and Cory stop the fighting in the bar. Then he turned to open the door to leave.

What was it? The hand on the shoulder, getting into Kyro's space? Was it possible that Art, using his vernacular from work when he broke up an argument, called him "brother"? What was it that lit the short fuse inside Kyro Sparks that at once set off all the cruelty, or self-hatred, or insecurity, or whatever diseased sense of himself as one badass son of a bitch that dwelled inside?

Kyro was on Art as he exited, grabbing hold of him in the narrow hallway. The door to the bar area was still shut. It was cramped; there was nowhere for Art to go. Either Kyro had to stop himself from what he had set in motion, or Art had to fight his way out.

"I'm not looking for any trouble," Art said.

Now Cory McLeod opened the door to the hallway, coming back to see what was taking Kyro so long. He saw some guy facing off with Kyro. That was what was happening, right? This guy was facing off against him? Cory knew that look in Kyro's face: he was hot. Cory just knew. It was on. You attacked one of them; you attacked them both. It was a rule. Anger popped inside Cory like a balloon bursting, then, unthinking, he rushed forward, punching, his vilest instincts exploding. Kyro was hitting Art, too; both were feeding off each other, raging, Art tried to get away, battle back, but there was nowhere to go. His hand grabbed the chain around Cory's neck, ripping it off. Art fell. He was down on the carpeted floor now — unable to stand up with the drinks, the fatigue, the two frenzied young men beating on him, unleashing a cruel cowardice that Art would never imagine could exist in a person. The fists. The boots. The shoes. Over and over, kicking and stomping. It was sickening. And over.

The door to the back hallway opened. It was a customer coming back from the bar. He saw a man slumped on the floor, on his knees, buttocks in the air, face on the floor, and the side of his head leaning against the wall. He saw two men over Art — and a third young man, holding open a door leading to a back alley. He saw one of the two men kick Art.

"Could you not do that, not kick him again?" the customer asked.

"Do you want some of this?" the man with metallic wire in his mouth asked.

"No."

The man kicked Art again, in the head, then they all moved toward the customer, and the door — the two men by the body, and the third who had held the back door. Kyro Sparks pushed the customer aside, and they were gone, out through the bar, the front door, walking, not running. They looked directly at the waitress, Cheryl, as they left. A couple of customers ran out the front door, saw the three of them starting to run along Upper James Street and around a corner. Another customer ran up to the bar.

"Art's being kicked by three guys," he said. Cheryl ran to the back hallway. "Art!" she screamed.

He did not respond. She wiped blood off his face. Art was breathing raspy, slow breaths. She felt his pulse. A faint one. Michelle, the bartender, called 911. It was 10:32 p.m.

"We need an ambulance to 592 Upper James Street in Hamilton. He's in the back hallway. We need an ambulance very quick."

She hung up. The 911 dispatch called the bar back.

"Are there any weapons involved?" dispatch asked.

"No. It was three black guys; they just left our bar. He's bleeding from the eyes — those three black guys beat the fuck out of him."

Michelle hurried toward Brenda on the dance floor. Brenda stopped dancing, moved to meet her; she could tell something was wrong.

"Art's been beat up. He's in the hallway. The ambulance is on the way."

Brenda ran to the back. Expected to find him there holding a bloody nose or sporting a black eye. She was not prepared to see him slumped on the floor.

"Art! Art!" She grabbed him, shouting his name, slapping the ground to get a reaction like she was taught when she updated her St. John Ambulance CPR training. She put her hand under his body, starting at the head, working down, looking for blood.

That's when uniform police officer Ian Gouthro appeared and helped her perform CPR. At 10:41 p.m. the paramedics came in the back door. More police arrived on the scene. Brenda was losing it; she was terrified. One of the officers physically lifted her away from Art to give the paramedics room, carrying her into the bar area. The music had stopped, the lights were on. Everyone was wondering what had happened. Art? In a fight? Brenda was numb. And angry. And helpless. What could she do?

She stood on a chair, shouting now. "If anyone finds these guys out there, bring them to my garage. I want a crack at them before the police."

Struggling to see what was happening, she noticed the defibrillator in the hallway near Art. But the paramedics were not using it. They were not using it to try to jump-start his heart, get him breathing. She knew that meant the worst. The boys. She had to get in touch with their sons. Neil and Jordan were a few blocks away at the house, getting ready to join their mom and dad at O'Grady's.

The phone rang. Bev picked up. She could tell that Brenda was calling from her cell. Unusual for her to do that, especially late in the evening like that. Bev didn't know where Brenda was; she did know Art and Brenda had gone out for dinner that night.

"Can you do something for me?" Brenda asked.

"What? What's the matter?" Bev said.

"Art's been beaten up."

"What?"

"Art's been beaten up and he's not breathing."

"So what the hell are you doing? Get him to the hospital!"

Brenda said that Art had been taken to the hospital. She needed Bev to go and bring the boys down to Hamilton General. Bev got off the phone and told her husband, Fred.

"Art? It can't be Art," he said. "Brenda must be mistaken. He must just be unconscious."

"Something is really wrong. This is bad."

A police cruiser drove Brenda from O'Grady's to the hospital. Aunt Bev and Uncle Fred arrived at the Rozendal's house just before 11:00 p.m. Jordan had just finished showering, getting ready to head out to the roadhouse. Neil was watching TV, waiting for his brother. Bev told them their dad was hurt, and at the hospital. They had to get down there and meet their mom.

Art had taught Neil to look for a smile or a laugh in any situation. In recent years they had lost several members of the extended family, most elderly, and Art always talked of the good times, made them laugh to help deal with it. At that moment Neil didn't want to believe the worst.

"What," Neil cracked, "did he trip and hit his head on the pool table or something?"

Bev said little. They rode to the hospital in silence. Fred parked, Bev hurried to the ER. She wanted to just make eye contact first. That's all she needed; she and Brenda were so close, the eyes would tell her all she needed to know. Bev spotted her. Brenda shook her head. Bev knew.

Paramedics had intubated Art at the bar, put a tube down his throat to assist breathing, given him epinephrine and atropine to try and restart the heart. It was no use. Art died at O'Grady's, before he arrived at the hospital, but paramedics do not officially declare death in the field. That would be up to the ER doctor.

At the General, Dr. John Opie was told by paramedics that Art had been VSA — vital signs absent — for about 40 minutes. His heart was asystole — no electric activity. Dr. Opie examined Art's pupils, felt his femoral artery in the groin for signs of a pulse. Nothing. He determined that resuscitation efforts would be futile. Art was pronounced dead at 11:14 p.m.

Brenda was not permitted to see Art's body, not when a homicide investigation surrounding his death had just begun. The body was evidence. The family gathered in the quiet room in the emergency department. How could Brenda tell Neil and Jordan? She wanted to start by telling them how proud Art was of them, use past-tense words, cushion the news in any way she could.

"You know, your dad loved you very much," Brenda began.

Before Brenda finished breaking the news, Neil asked what had happened to his dad.

An ER staffer in the room turned and said, "He's dead."

At that moment Jordan opened the door and bolted from the room and out of the ER, the others following him. He ran outside, down Barton Street, escaping, trying to run from the news. Someone chased him down. Neil stayed back, outside the hospital, sat on a cement wall, and wept.

Art's mother, Frances, arrived at the hospital and so did Art's sister, Debbie. A police officer took Brenda and Neil to Central Station to meet homicide Detective Mike Maloney. Bev and the others took a cab.

"Where to?" the cabbie asked.

"The police station on King William," Bev said. "And if any of your cabbies picked up anyone in the Upper James and Brucedale area tonight, the police would really like to know about it. Because my brother-in-law was beaten to death tonight."

The cabbie dropped them off at the station and waived the fare. He sent flowers to the funeral. The card was simply signed, "The taxi cab driver."

After several hours at Central Station, a police officer drove Brenda and Neil home, where they rejoined family members gathered at the house. At 6:00 a.m., the city dark and cold, Brenda, exhausted and wired, picked up the phone. She had calls to make.

7

A GRUESOME DISCOVERY

Saturday morning the phone rang on the nightstand beside Bill Murray's bed. He was supposed to come to Art and Brenda's place for dinner that night.

"Brenda, what's up?" he said, barely awake.

She felt numb. It was all so surreal. Brenda spoke evenly.

"You're not going to believe what's happened," she began.

Bill was thinking that maybe Art had been called in to work, and that dinner was off. But why call him at six in the morning?

"Art's been beaten up and he died."

"Brenda, where is your head?" Bill said, unable to compute the words. She repeated it. And now he believed. Almost at that exact moment, his kids, aged 14 and 10, walked in the bedroom awakened by the phone. The kids loved Art. Bill didn't know what to say to them. What else could he say, but relay the news? It shook the kids up bad.

Bill moped around all day, cried on and off, mostly just unable to make sense of it. His friendship with Art was the kind that if one of them had some idea, for a car, anything, one would instantly call the other. For the longest time after he heard the news, a thought would cross Bill's mind, and he'd actually reach for the phone but had to stop himself. I can't call him. Art is gone.

Art's brother Darren was now living up north, in Ironbridge. That morning Darren heard the knock at his front door and answered in his housecoat. It was his mom, standing in the doorway with a panicked look on her face.

"There's been an accident," she said.

"What?"

Thoughts rushed through Darren's mind — perhaps his stepfather, Neil, had had another heart attack. Esther kept looking at Darren, opening her mouth to speak, but she couldn't say the words.

Darren was almost shouting now. "What — just tell me!"

"Art was killed last night."

"What — how?"

"He was beaten up in a bar."

Darren turned from her, barely made it to the bathroom and vomited, then he cried, hard. He showered, still crying, the news ripping his heart, torturing his head. It all made no sense. Beaten up? In a bar? Art could never be in a fight, never bring anything onto himself. Darren? Sure. He knew that he could get himself into a situation. No question about it. Not Art. Ever. A bar fight? How was it possible? How could anyone ever want to hurt Art? *It should have been me*, Darren thought. *Should have been me in that bar.* Not that he wanted to die, but his brother meant so much to others — had a wife, kids, all these people who love him. Art's sister, Debbie, came north and drove Darren, Neil, and Esther back to Hamilton. All those years before, when he was still a little boy, Darren had gone on that long drive south to Hamilton to see Art. He was doing it again, to attend the funeral.

On Saturday morning, just after 10:30 a.m., the body was wheeled from the sealed morgue fridge in the basement of Hamilton General Hospital into the autopsy room. At 10:40 a.m. forensic pathologist Dr. John Fernandes began the post-mortem examination. Fernandes had performed more than 1,200 forensic autopsies in his career, 90 of them homicides. Also in the room was Kevin Stanley, a detective representing the homicide investigation. Stanley opened his white casebook and made notes. Fernandes spoke aloud as he proceeded, making observations that would appear in his final report: "Male, 43 years old. Height: five feet, 9.7 inches. Weight: 198 lb. Body habitus: Lean, muscular. Scalp & facial hair: Brown-red. Brown-red moustache. Extremities: Hands covered by dry brown paper bags. Hands stained with grease in many of the creases reflective of industrial-type staining of the hands ... Gold tone ring with a single colourless stone on the left fourth finger."

Kevin Stanley had attended many autopsies in the past. With this one he strained to keep his professional instincts tuned to the job at hand. He was an emotional guy, known to wear his heart on his sleeve. He couldn't help but think of his own family: he had been married to the same woman for years; was a father of two boys — just like Art Rozendal. He could see himself being in the same situation as Art. Out for dinner with the family, and then it just happens: your life is extinguished just like that. Senseless.

Fernandes ordered X-rays, noted injuries around the head, neck, and chest, swelling and bruising around both eyes. The left cheek was swollen and discoloured. Scratches on the left eyebrow. Right ear extensively bruised. Bruising around the left rib cage measuring 10 x 12 centimetres. His attention was drawn to marks on the skin on Art's back. There appeared to be a circular pattern to them. He knew that studying trauma patterns on tissue can be instructive about the cause of death.

At 1:40 p.m. he halted the autopsy. He wanted to see the marks more clearly. Allowing time to pass would allow the bruising on the back to develop more clearly. In the meantime Fernandes wanted to visit the scene of the beating, look for anything that could have produced that kind of pattern on Art Rozendal's back. While Stanley stood guard at the morgue, another officer drove the forensic pathologist up to O'Grady's.

Forensic detectives Gary Zwicker and Annette Huys were there, and they walked Fernandes through the bar. He briefly examined the hallway where Art had died. Doorknob? Obstruction of some kind protruding from the wall? There was nothing in that hallway that could have made such a pattern on the back. The doctor returned to the hospital. At 4:20 p.m. the body was sealed again in the morgue freezer.

Back at O'Grady's that afternoon and into the evening, Huys and Zwicker continued processing the scene. They measured the back hallway and bathroom and other portions of the bar. Zwicker drew a detailed scale diagram of the entire layout inside. The roadhouse was laid bare in the harsh light of day, empty, the air stale. O'Grady's was non-smoking, but clearly the rules were lax. The detectives collected cigarette butts in the back hallway for saliva DNA. They dusted the door leading to the back hallway and the bathroom walls for prints. But the walls were grimy; there were few quality prints to be had. They photographed and tagged items that might have been handled by the three men witnesses had seen leaving the bar, such as pool cues and balls. Huys opened a container of sterilized water, popped the cap on a tube, drew an amulet, dabbed it in the water and rubbed the rim of a drinking glass. She returned the swab to its container and attached a seal.

All of the samples would be sent to the Centre of Forensic Sciences in Toronto. She placed used drinking straws from the glasses in sealed envelopes for delivery to CFS — and noted which end had been the drinking end. Huys had learned that one from experience — she once got a note back from CFS on one case asking which end of the straw was which. Among the items to be sent for DNA testing was a neck chain found on the floor of the hallway right where the beating took place. Uniform officer Ian Gouthro had been the first to notice it when he reported to the scene. It was a dirty silver chain with a dog tag. There was an inscription on the tag. It read: Daymein P.

On Monday, at 8:05 a.m., Dr. Fernandes re-examined the bruising on Art's back. The pattern was clearer now: "Patterned injuries noted to the central portion of the back and on the left flank.... Contusion pattern in centre of back measuring six x five centimetres. Pattern appears as a series of somewhat circular lines with intervening zones of sparing around which there appeared to be a radiating pattern of lines perpendicular to the outermost circle." The marks on the skin, he concluded, "had the appearance of a pattern commonly seen on the soles of shoes or boots."

Holding his homicide notebook, Det. Kevin Stanley leaned over the body and examined the marks. A gruesome discovery. The tread marks were visceral proof of the brutality of the attack. Someone had stomped on the back so hard that it made an impression through his shirt and into the skin. Stanley, a cop for 24 years, had never seen anything like it. Stanley drew a sketch of the circular pattern in his notebook.

With Kyro Sparks held at Barton Street jail, Det. Mike Maloney pursued leads and tips coming in from officers in the field in the hunt for other suspects. One man had called police concerned that his son might have been at O'Grady's that night — he was worried his son played a role. Turned out to be a dead end. He also drove to the east end station to meet a 26-year-old man who had been arrested for carrying a concealed weapon — a large kitchen knife up his sleeve. Another dead end. At two that afternoon, Maloney drove to the hospital and headed to the morgue.

The forensic pathologist had finished his examination, which meant the body was about to be released by police to the Rozendal family.

Maloney was among those who tried to talk Brenda out of seeing Art's body in the morgue. He always urged families of homicide victims not to do it. Family members wanted to see their loved one right away, but the morgue's hangover effect could often end up hurting them more in the long run, he felt. One woman told Maloney she never got over that experience in the bowels of the General — the long walk down the hallway to the morgue, the pungent smell of bleach and other odours. The markings from the beating were still pronounced. Maloney urged Brenda to wait and see Art once the body had been prepared in the funeral home. Liz Repchuck, manager of victim services with Hamilton Police, also advised her against viewing in the morgue.

Brenda knew everyone was trying to protect her. But didn't they understand? She had been the one there when he died. She needed to be with him again.

"I want to see him," she said. "And it is my right."

Up at the Rozendal house, family had gathered, supporting one another — among them Darren, and Art's dad, Neil, his mom, Frances, sisters Debbie and Sandi. Neil said he wanted to come down to the morgue with Brenda, too. Brenda tried talking him out of it. Neil Rozendal was 71 and had a serious heart condition — one heart attack and bypass surgery three times — and had not seen what Brenda had that night.

"You don't want to see your son that way," she said.

It was not a long conversation.

"I'm going," Neil said.

At the morgue Art's father and wife were advised not to touch the body, not in its current state. The funeral home would be a better place for that. Brenda, Neil, Mike Maloney, and Liz Repchuck stood at the viewing window. A curtain over the glass parted. Art's body lay on a table, a sheet covering him up to his neck. They stood and watched for a couple of minutes in silence. It wasn't enough. Brenda and Neil wanted to get closer. They were escorted into the room, walked up close, leaned over his face. Brenda desperately wanted to touch him. Art's dad Neil could not hold back. He held his boy's hand, kissed his fingers, and held them against his cheek.

"I love you," he said.

8

WHITE HEAT

POLICE CHARGE ONE, HUNT TWO OTHERS IN MOUNTAIN MURDER. That was the headline on the front page of Monday's *Hamilton Spectator*. Peter Abi-Rashed, the investigation case manager, had spoken to a reporter from the newspaper. At this early stage in the case, exposure in the media could only help to encourage tips from the public; it might even convince the other men involved in the attack to come forward. Abi-Rashed, a burly cop with a booming voice, was not one for beating around the bush.

"Get a lawyer and come on in," Abi-Rashed was quoted in the story. "Because it's only a matter of time before we come after you."

Brenda Rozendal was also quoted: "If there's somebody out there with more information, please come forward. There were a lot of people at the place we were at. There's got to be somebody who saw more."

The detectives knew that Kyro Sparks was not a perfect suspect. He had admitted nothing and refused to even be interviewed. Eyewitness accounts of the man with the silver grills in his mouth kicking Art in the head, daring a customer to intervene, and leaving the bar, were damning, certainly — but not all of the witnesses at O'Grady's had been able to pick Sparks out of a photo lineup. In addition Sparks's post-offence conduct had been bizarre. Maloney and Abi-Rashed discussed it. Why was Sparks still in the area of the homicide an hour after the offence? If he had just murdered somebody, why would he hang around with police crawling around everywhere? Made no sense. The detectives had to pose the question: Do we have the right guy?

Still, assuming Sparks was one of Art Rozendal's killers, he might hold the key to catching the other two. Maloney studied Sparks's criminal record. It included robbery, drug possession for the purpose of trafficking, assaulting a peace officer. He was convicted for extortion in 2001. For that incident Waterloo police had charged him with use of firearm during commission of an offence, which was later withdrawn. He had also been flagged by Waterloo police as having a "street gang association." Might he have been out with gang members at O'Grady's?

Maloney put out a "zone alert" to other police services. It included details of the Rozendal homicide, descriptions of the suspects, and background on Kyro Sparks. Detective Constable Ben Hadfield of Waterloo Intelligence Gang Unit sent an email in response. The note said Kyro Sparks had been on an "observation category" with police. And Hadfield passed along names of known associates of Sparks. The first of four names read: Cory McLeod. DOB: 1985/April 20. Last known address: Kitchener. Nicknames: Spits. Exile. King Dama. Daymein.

On Monday afternoon the body was moved from the hospital to the Clark funeral home on Upper Wellington Street and prepared for the funeral. When Brenda had first viewed Art's body, she felt conflicting emotions. She told Art she loved him, but she also felt anger, told him she was mad at him for dying on her. But sitting alone with him in the funeral home, it was different. Brenda ran her fingers through Art's hair, fixed it — they had not made it up quite right, she decided. She cried, and she kissed him. His lips felt cold against hers.

Prior to the visitation, Brenda allowed her two sisters, Bev and Diane, to view Art's body in the funeral home, but denied others in the family a chance to see it. She decided that there would be a closed casket. Clark's had made him up as best as possible, but the bruising was still visible and his eyes were swollen. The fact that he had been in the morgue for a couple of days did not help. Brenda didn't want the family to remember him like that. Art and Brenda's sons, Neil and Jordan, both wanted to see him, but she refused. Bev and Diane later told her that they regretted seeing the body and had nightmares about it.

The visitation was on Wednesday, January 19. It snowed and the wind chill hit minus 16 degrees Celsius that morning. Despite the cold people lined up outside the funeral home right around the block. Among those offering condolences was Mike Maloney and the other homicide detectives. Nancy Lutz was there, a uniform officer who had driven Brenda to the hospital that night. So was Ian Gouthro, who had been first on the scene. The two officers walked up to greet her together.

"Here are my angels," Brenda said.

"No, you are the angel."

Gouthro looked at Brenda. He was not a talkative guy, but he just sensed that he needed to say it. She struck him as a very strong woman. Heroic. He felt she needed to know.

"You did everything possible to save your husband," he said. "I want you to know that."

Art had been beaten, but Brenda did not know the official cause of his death. The detectives didn't know, either — they were waiting on the final post-mortem report. Brenda had wondered: did she do something wrong when she tried to revive Art? Performed CPR incorrectly? Gouthro's words now brought some comfort. But it was difficult to focus any of her thoughts or feelings.

The next day about 200 people attended the funeral presided over Rev. John Hibbs, who had married Art and Brenda and helped them renew their vows.

"Art had a great sense of humour, unique one-liners and a distinctive laugh," he told the congregation. "Art had a hug and a kiss for everyone, even me. He loved people."

The crime against him, Hibbs said, was hard to comprehend for anybody with "a common humanity, decency and respect for life." But do not dwell upon the forces that took him. "We will leave justice to be done to others."

Debbie, one of Art's younger sisters, also spoke. She talked of her brother's love of cars and animals. "Art was there when I opened my eyes for the first time," she said, tears in her eyes. "I thought he would be there when I closed my eyes for the last time. There was a change in plans."

All of Art's co-workers at Stelco attended, too. The flag flying outside Stelco was lowered to half-mast. All the guys were in shock. How could anyone want to hurt Art of all people? Art's locker remained packed with his gear. His white helmet, dusty and tarnished, the one with his name on it, still hung from a hook on the wall. No one touched it.

Charlie Montgomery was there, as well. He had spent two years working with him on the same shift and had grown very close. You work in a heavy industrial environment, you have to trust the other guy with your life, trust him to do the right thing. He could always trust Art.

Montgomery had been to many funerals over the years, his parents never hid death from them when they were kids. When his great aunts and uncles had died, their funerals were celebrations of life. Charlie spoke at his dad's funeral. People asked him, where he had found the strength. Death is part of life, he had explained. Charlie could handle death, but not this time. It was too much; he could make no sense of it. Sitting in the church with everyone, maybe it was because he was trying to understand, or keep his emotions in check, but sitting there Charlie felt this ... this fever, this white heat wrapped around his head the whole time.

Something strange happened at the burial — it seemed unreal, but several people saw it, and that included Art's buddy Bill Murray. Bill wasn't into paranormal stuff or anything like that. But he saw what he saw. There they all were in Woodlands Cemetery, freezing cold, snow falling on and off, the burial service underway, and Reverend Hibbs speaking, family and close friends gathered around the casket. Midway through the service, though, Bill turned, and there it was: a car stopped nearby on the narrow driveway that winds through the cemetery. Bill couldn't believe his eyes. It was a street rod, a 1968 Buick Gran Sport, mint shape. Just like the kind Bill and Art used to put up on blocks and restore. No one drove a car like that in winter, he thought. Ever. You brought it out in summer, if the weather was perfect. Guys didn't even drive them in rain, much less through snow or salt. But there it was. A Gran Sport, Art's favourite. And it was white, of all things, with blacked tinted windows.

Bill thought he could see someone get out of the car, but he couldn't see a face; the car blocked his view. And then, seconds later, the car glided away, the engine barely audible, if at all. Bill knew every car guy around, and he had never seen anyone with a car like that. Bill asked Art's old friends about it. No one knew who it could have been. Never did find out.

9

"I HATE COPS"

Mike Maloney now had a list of possible Kitchener-based friends of Kyro Sparks. But had any of them been with Sparks at O'Grady's? If Sparks was living or working in Hamilton, he could have an entirely different set of associates in the city. He needed more. Tips were flowing in, sightings of men in the area near O'Grady's on Upper James Street the night of the homicide.

Maloney reflected that when a solid citizen was murdered, there was always lots of information that came in from the people who had cared about the victim. When it was someone living on the fringe in Hamilton, that was not the case. In that sense Art Rozendal's reputation was actually helping the investigation into his death.

The second investigator in the Rozendal homicide was Greg Jackson, a broad-shouldered detective who stood six foot two and weighed in at 210 pounds; he looked like he could play receiver for the Ticats. Policing in Hamilton ran in Jackson's family. His late father, Cliff, had been a cop. So, too, had his grandfather, Ernie. As a boy Jackson remembered seeing Ernie at the old Criminal Investigations Division, a dusty office that looked like the set from the *Barney Miller* TV show.

Jackson viewed notes taken by uniform officers who had reported to the scene at O'Grady's Roadhouse, and witness statements taken in the early hours of the investigation. Most homicide scenes in Hamilton are populated by few people; a crowded bar was a different matter. It meant more legwork for investigators, but was also a great advantage in learning what had happened and who might have been involved. Every eye holds a tiny piece of the puzzle. What did they see?

Jackson called in more than a dozen witnesses to provide statements or expand on those already given to police. Jackson, Maloney, and the other detectives would eventually interview about 45 people who had been there the night of the murder. The killers had by all accounts simply walked out the front door, out onto Upper James Street. One suspect had been arrested in the area — but what about the others?

Maloney interviewed a cabbie who said he gave a ride that night to a fare that fitted Kyro Sparks's description. The fare had been rude to him, called him a "Paki," spat and swore at him. An interesting bit of detail: the guy also mentioned that he had a girlfriend in town who went to Mohawk College. The cabbie — who had once been a major in the Pakistani army — ordered the guy out of the cab.

The cabbie added that he had picked up the guy in front of the Double Double Pizza on Upper James Street. Maloney went to the pizza place, asked if they had a working video camera on site that night. They did not. The Mohawk tip was something, though. The detectives worked through Mohawk College, posted notices on campus about the crime, suggesting that a suspect may have visited a student in residence there. Reward for information was offered: $2,000. Jackson interviewed a woman who cut hair on campus, who said she had a customer who fitted the description of one of the suspects offered up by police. The lead did not pan out.

Maloney reviewed another Crime Stoppers tip. It was from a customer who had been shopping at a No Frills store at Mohawk and Upper James Street, on Friday, January 14, around 2:00 p.m. Art was killed that night. The tip described two men in the store "not really shopping, just pushing a buggy around and watching the customers." One of them fitted Sparks's description. The other "had an afro with pony tail and a white pick (comb) sticking out of his hair. Navy blue puffy hip length winter coat, five-eleven, slim build, no facial hair." Maloney was impressed — pretty good description from a customer who just happened to be shopping there. In a perfect world, the No Frills store would have working video cameras. He phoned the store.

"How long do you keep your security tapes for?"

"Three months," the manager said.

On Wednesday morning, January 19, Maloney drove to the store and watched a section of the video. Between 2:07 p.m. and 2:30 p.m., he saw two males on camera pushing the buggy. It was the first video tape of many. Peter Abi-Rashed ordered officers to retrieve every store video in that part of Upper James Street. Viewing the No Frills video was simple enough because the tip had specified what time of day to look at. For the rest of them, it meant viewing recordings from around January 14 from start to finish. A constable named Sarah Watson was seconded to view hundreds of hours of footage.

That same day Maloney put in a phone call to the Barton Street jail. Kyro Sparks's known associates had been in trouble with police in the past. Might one of them actually be in jail? The jail had access to data listing the names of every person currently housed in a detention centre in Ontario. An official told Maloney that one of Sparks's friends, the one named Cory McLeod, was currently incarcerated at Maplehurst institution in Milton. Clearly, Cory McLeod would not have had opportunity to attack Art Rozendal if he was in jail already. Except McLeod had turned himself in to Kitchener police on an aggravated assault and weapons charge on January 15 — the day after Art was killed. He appeared in court three days later and was taken to Maplehurst not long after that. Cory McLeod had been a free man at the time Art was killed. But if he was involved in the homicide, why would he turn himself in? The detectives talked about it. McLeod was hiding in jail. Had to be. After the homicide the guy had figured that he would take off for Kitchener, out of the Hamilton Police jurisdiction. He could turn himself in, hide out in jail, and let the dust settle. Wait for his assault beef in Kitchener to be dealt with, then take off. Police weren't going to look for a murder suspect in prison.

Maloney knew they didn't have to immediately visit McLeod at Maplehurst. Not yet. He wasn't going anywhere. What they needed was evidence putting him in Hamilton at the time of the homicide. On Thursday, January 20, Maloney phoned a security officer at Maplehurst. What personal effects did Cory McLeod have with him? The officer said McLeod had white Nike running shoes, a black ski jacket, grey sweater, beige pants. Maloney passed along the information to the Hamilton constable reviewing the store videotapes.

On Tuesday, January 25, at 9:30 a.m., Maloney called the security manager at Barton Street jail. He asked if inmate Kyro Sparks had received any visitors lately. He had two visitors who came to see him on January 17, and January 19. Names: Katrina McLennan and Sherri Foreman, both of 643 Upper James Street, apartment 2. In the register, Sherri had written "friend," Katrina wrote "girlfriend." Maloney called Maplehurst. Cory McLeod had not been receiving visitors. Letters? He had not received any letters — but he had mailed out letters of his own. He had written two females who lived in Meaford, Ontario, and there was a letter he mailed to a woman in Hamilton. The name written on the envelope was "Sherri McLeod," and the address was 643 Upper James Street, apartment 2. Cory McLeod and Kyro Sparks both had a Hamilton connection. Their girlfriends lived in the apartment around the corner from O'Grady's Roadhouse.

At 8:20 the next morning, Wednesday, an anonymous caller left a message on Maloney's voicemail: "I think I might know who one of your suspects is from Kitchener," the caller said. He said he knew Kyro Sparks, and that Kyro hung out with a guy named Cory McLeod. Said the guy had a big afro and put his hair in a ponytail.

"Cory is the type of guy that snaps when he gets drunk. He brags about it. Brags about killing someone." The caller added he was offering the information because "the guy they killed was a contributor, a millwright. And now his kids are orphaned."

At 10:00 a.m. Maloney and Detective Greg Jackson checked out an unmarked car and drove to 643 Upper James. They knocked at apartment 2. No answer. Someone moved a drape in the window. They were there all right. Maloney knocked again. No answer.

The detectives entered a sewing shop at the front of the building. A woman there said her husband was the building superintendent. apartment 2? Tenant was a girl named Katrina. She was a student at Mohawk College, but was from Kitchener. Her parents were really nice people. Back at apartment 2, the woman knocked on the door for the detectives, while Maloney and Jackson stood off to the side out of view. Katrina opened the door. When the detectives stepped out, she looked surprised — and did not invite them in. Maloney and Jackson stepped inside. Sherri Foreman was sitting in the room.

"We're investigating a murder at O'Grady's Roadhouse," Maloney said. "A man named Kyro Sparks has been arrested. We have information that he's been here." He said nothing about Cory McLeod.

In fact the detectives had no information that put Sparks in that apartment. But they had a strong suspicion. An eyewitness at the bar who had followed the killers outside O'Grady's said they had hopped a fence near that building. Sherri said they both knew Kyro from Kitchener, but added that he had not been in their apartment on Upper James Street. Guys come by the apartment, she said, but he was not one of them. The detectives warned them: "This is a murder investigation. Obstruct police and we will arrest you."

"We'd like to talk to you down at the station," Jackson said.

They left the building and got in the car; the detectives drove them down the Mountain. Better to take Katrina and Sherri downtown, interview them separately, and get statements from each on the record, on videotape.

"How long have you known Kyro Sparks?" Maloney asked to start the interview.

"I don't know," Katrina replied.

As the camera rolled, Greg Jackson transcribed. Sherri Foreman waited in the hallway.

"Are you Kyro's girlfriend?"

"No."

"How did you sign in at the jail to visit him?"

"Girlfriend."

Maloney asked her about January 14, the night of the homicide at O'Grady's Roadhouse on Upper James Street.

"Do you remember the night it happened? It was Friday night, a week ago last Friday."

"I honestly don't know about that."

"Do you recall where you were that Friday night?"

"At my place?"

"Were you there or are you not sure?"

"I'm not sure."

"Can you guess when the last time was that Kyro was at your place? I'm trying to assist you in recollecting the last time he was there."

"Who said he was there? You have people telling you that he's been there? Did I not tell you how many black guys came to my house? How do you know one was Kyro?"

"I don't."

"So how are you going to believe these people?"

"Are you telling me Kyro has never been to your house?

"Hmm."

"Is that a no? He has or hasn't?"

"I met him in Kitchener."

Maloney told her at least two guys left O'Grady's that night and were seen by a witness heading toward the apartment.

"Did anyone come to your apartment that night? Did anyone come to your place and say, 'I can't believe what happened; I just beat up a guy in a bar?'"

She giggled.

"What's so funny?"

"Oh, I don't know."

"It's not funny. Someone got killed. If that was your father, I don't think you'd be laughing."

"I know. I don't think it's funny; I just laugh all the time. It's just me. You say the most serious thing and I'll laugh."

"What does Kyro think about all this?"

"I don't know. Ask him."

"Do your parents know that Kyro is a friend of yours and has been arrested for murder? What would they say?"

"Why are you going to involve my parents?"

"I'm not involving them; I'm just wondering. What would your parents think?"

"I don't know; they probably wouldn't be too happy. But he hasn't been found guilty."

Maloney told Katrina she may end up on the stand in court and be asked by a defence lawyer to provide an alibi for Kyro for his whereabouts that night.

"I know, it's a big show. I know what goes on."

"You know what goes on."

"Uh-huh."

It was Sherri Foreman's turn. Maloney was careful to not mention Cory McLeod's name. He knew McLeod had been in contact with Sherri.

"How long have you known Kyro Sparks?"

Hamilton Police Service.

09-MAR-09   10:51-23

Sherri Foreman and Katrina McLennan were interrogated by police.

"I don't even know how long I've known him, I've just met him a couple of times."

"When?"

"I don't know, I just met him in Kitchener. I don't know when."

"When?"

"It was warm out."

"Warm out?"

"Summer. That's all I know."

Maloney asked what she was doing the night of the homicide.

"Probably was in Kitchener. Or even Hamilton. I don't remember that far back."

"I want to explain something to you, Sherri," Maloney said. "There's a thing called accessory after the fact. That means if someone committed the crime and afterward you didn't even know they committed the crime, but you assisted them hiding in your apartment or something like that, you could be charged. It's a very serious crime."

"I know, I've heard of that."

"So you didn't do anything like that; no one came saying, 'Hey, can we stay here a while?'"

"I'd be, like, 'Get out of my house.'"

"You know if someone has obstructed us, this isn't a little shoplift; someone's life was taken. This is a murder. If someone has lied to us, we will charge them criminally."

"Yeah, I'm aware of that."

"And everything you have told me here today is the truth?"

"Yeah."

The interviews over, Katrina and Sherri waited in the hallway for the detectives to take them home.

"I hate fucking cops," Sherri said, loud enough for Jackson to hear.

10

A KILLER'S SHOES

On Tuesday, February 1, the instructor walked into the classroom at Mohawk College at 8:00 a.m. He was an older guy, Katrina thought, but cute. Had some kind of accent. The class started. Katrina wrote the date on her notepad, and began: "Hey baby, how are you doing? Me, I'm tired …"

Katrina took courses at Mohawk in business, commerce, psychology, popular culture, sociology. She had fared poorly in all of them. They had a test coming up today, after the break. She was ready to fail it. What was the instructor talking about, she wondered? Didn't understand a single word the dude was saying. She continued her letter to Kyro Sparks. "Hope he doesn't ask me a question. Because for sure I won't know the answer LOL.…"

After writing the test, she wrote: "Don't know how I did, but filled in all the answers LOL. I have a hangnail on my thumb and it hurts." She wrote to Kyro that after classes she was going back to the apartment to tidy things up with Sherri, rearrange some stuff: "I have some bad news, wish I could tell you in person. When I came home this weekend my parents decided it would be best if I got out of Hamilton. I have people watching me like fucking crazy.… Baby I want you to know that I'm not abandoning you, I would never do that. If it was that easy I wouldn't be so sad. This is going to be just as hard for you as it is for me, but you have to still try and be good in there. When you get mad please don't do something stupid.…"

She was having a tough time, she told Kyro — trouble sleeping, lying awake every night, thinking about stuff. During the day it all made her want to cry: "Please try not to think of bad things and try to be happy.

And if not, then just don't do what you know what I don't want you doing while you're in there.... I almost didn't want to tell you all this because I was scared how you'd react. But whatever you think, just please don't think that I won't be there for you, because I always will be ..."

On Wednesday, February 2, forensic detective Annette Huys visited Waterloo police. There she compared a fingerprint she'd lifted from one of the drinking glasses at O'Grady's to prints Waterloo had on file for Cory McLeod. They matched.

The next day Maloney and Jackson also visited Waterloo police. They showed video stills from the No Frills store on Upper James recorded January 14 — the day of the killing — to a police officer and a Kitchener social worker who were both familiar with McLeod. The officer confirmed one of the males on the video was McLeod. The social worker said he was "110 percent sure that it is Cory McLeod."

The detectives left the station. At 4:45 p.m. they visited Sherri Foreman's home in Kitchener. Her mother was there. They said nothing about Cory McLeod.

"We have a suspect named Kyro Sparks in custody for a murder in Hamilton," Maloney said. "We believe he has been associating with your daughter and her friend."

They asked where Sherri had been around the time of the homicide. Her mother said she was unsure if her daughter had been at home in Kitchener on January 14 or 15. She'd never heard of Sparks before, but said Sherri had had a friend to the house the summer before named Cory. Just after 5:00 p.m., the detectives visited Katrina's house and spoke to her mother. She said she had never heard of Kyro Sparks, and didn't know where Katrina had been the weekend of January 14-16.

"Your daughter and Sherri Foreman visited Kyro in jail," Maloney said. "I think your daughter and Sherri are not telling us the whole truth."

Maloney knew they needed a crack at searching the girls' apartment in Hamilton; they needed to look for evidence that Sparks, McLeod, and the third guy had been there the night Art was killed. But they still had no legal grounds for obtaining a search warrant. They had proof the girls visited and exchanged letters with Sparks and McLeod in jail. It wasn't enough to get a warrant. If Katrina permanently vacated the apartment, however, that was a different matter.

On Monday, February 7, Maloney called Katrina's parents. They told him their daughter was moving back home. This was their chance.

"We have to get up there," Maloney told Jackson. "Time it when they are moving; maybe we can get consent to search."

Wednesday morning Jackson and Det. Kevin Stanley dropped by the apartment on Upper James Street to see if Katrina was still there. The landlord said she had moved out the day before. Her dad had helped her. The father had been quite apologetic that she was breaking her lease.

The detectives asked the landlord if he would mind if they looked around the apartment? Jackson and Stanley entered apartment number 2. There was a shopping bag left on the floor. A No Frills bag. Nothing in it. The rest of the place was empty.

"They took some garbage bags out back," the landlord said.

Out behind the building, they saw four green garbage bags. They loaded them in the backseat of their unmarked white cruiser and headed to Central Station. The detectives had been on the job too long, seen too much, sorted through too much garbage, to be overly enthused by the discovery. Stanley worked vice and drugs for six years — seizing garbage bags was standard procedure.

Real investigative work is not like *CSI* on TV — every search does not blow a case open. If you're lucky, you might get one eureka moment like that in your career, where X really does mark the spot. Jackson and Stanley had already had theirs about five months earlier, investigating a stabbing homicide. One day Jackson suggested they check the roofs of buildings near where a witness had last seen the killer downtown. They climbed a ladder atop the first roof. Bingo: there was a bag containing a pair of jeans. Blood all over them. Victim's blood on the outside, killer's DNA inside. Case closed.

At 11:30 a.m. Maloney answered his phone in the office. It was Jackson calling from the car. "We found four garbage bags out back of the girls' apartment," Jackson said.

Maloney was unimpressed. More garbage. Great, he mused. Was the garbage even hers? It was possible, Jackson replied.

Maloney met the detectives in the basement garage at Central. Maloney and Stanley slipped on rubber gloves, opened the bags. One of the first items in the bag was an empty Timberlands shoe box. Interesting.

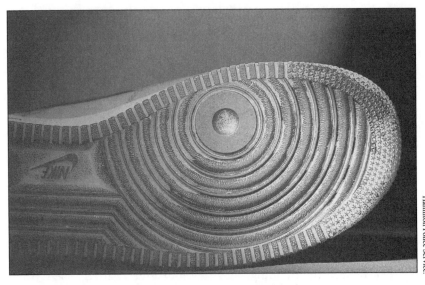

Police matched the tread on this shoe to an imprint on Art's back.

Kyro Sparks wore Timberlands. There was another pair of shoes, called Lugz. Phone bills, cable bills.

After opening the second bag Stanley noticed a pair of Nike running shoes, tanned colour. He held one shoe. Turned it over. Unbelievable. The tread. In his mind's eye, he saw the drawing in his homicide case book. The circular pattern. The marks on Art Rozendal's back the forensic pathologist showed him in the morgue. A killer's shoes.

"These are the shoes!" he shouted. "These are the shoes, no doubt about it — these are the ones." He put down the shoe, grabbed his notebook, turned to the page where he had illustrated the markings, showed the others. "Look at this. Look at it."

Maloney took charge. "Let's hold it guys; let's just pause here."

They needed to preserve the integrity of the evidence, record what they had, by the numbers, step by step. Get forensics in there to take pictures and secure it.

Annette Huys took the call in the forensic identification department. It was Stanley on the line. He told her she might want to come to the garage and take a look at something. They had a present for her. And bring your camera. In the garage Huys saw the tread. She had seen the autopsy photos. X marks the spot.

The back hallway of O'Grady's, where Art Rozendal was beaten to death.

Huys noticed a tiny dark spot on the left shoe. Might be blood. She could not use a Hemastix strip to test it on the spot; the sample was too small, almost a misting. The chemical from the Hemastix might compromise it. Better to seal the shoes for testing at the Centre of Forensic

Sciences in Toronto. If it was blood, whose blood was it? Just as important, who wore the shoe? Could they find DNA inside it? Not if the person wore socks, reflected Huys.

The DNA test was critical. After Huys had packaged the shoes, Kevin Stanley hit the Queen Elizabeth Way and drove the evidence to the CFS. The next day Alexandra Welsh in the biology section of CFS sent a fax to Maloney. She had finished analysis on the O'Grady's drinking glasses. The DNA profile developed from a swab of one of the glasses matched the DNA profile on record for Cory McLeod. As a convicted offender, McLeod's profile had previously been registered on a national database.

Maloney met with case manager Peter Abi-Rashed, Greg Jackson, and assistant Crown attorney Joe Nadel to discuss where the case might be heading. One suspect — Sparks — in custody; another — McLeod — in the works. Witnesses had told the detectives about a third guy who was also in that back hallway in O'Grady's where Art died, and who had held the back door open. His identity was still a mystery.

They had forensic evidence proving that Sparks and McLeod drank from glasses in the bar the night of the homicide. A witness had described three young men with Art in the back hallway, including a man resembling Sparks kicking Art in the head. But did they have direct evidence that would be enough to prove in court that Sparks, McLeod, and the mystery third guy had been the ones who killed Art? Could they establish intent? The kick to the head? The tread marks on Art's back? Could they prove who wore the shoes?

The DNA results were one key, and so was the final post-mortem report from Dr. John Fernandes, the forensic pathologist. What was it, specifically, that had caused Art's death?

Two weeks later, on February 25, Maloney received a phone call from Alexandra Welsh. She told him she had preliminary results from the shoes found in the garbage bag. Tiny blood stains were detected on the Lugz shoes — but the amount was insufficient to analyze. They could not even tell if the blood was human or animal.

What about the misting on the Nikes? Welsh had tested the substance found on the exterior of the right shoe. It tested positive for blood. Art Rozendal's blood. The probability that it was not his was 1 in 4.6 billion. The second part of the equation still remained. Who wore it?

11

THREE KINGS

Brenda Rozendal's eyes stared emptily out the window. The stone for Art's burial plot in Woodland Cemetery had not yet been put in, so she sat in her parked van, out of the cold, looking at the spot where it would eventually go. She awoke early most every day, alone but for the denim shirt in bed with her. The shirt was Art's. At bedtime each night, Brenda pulled one of his work shirts out of the closet and held it close to her under the covers.

Each morning she picked up a cup of apple-cinnamon tea and parked by his plot, along the winding road in the cemetery. She lit a cigarette, alone with her thoughts. Sometimes, if the detectives had called her with updates on the investigation, she would walk over to the plot and tell Art the latest news.

Brenda felt a bond with the detectives; she loved those guys. But she was anxious for the police to arrest the others who had beat up Art. It was coming up on two months since he was killed. Bev, Brenda's sister, was not shy reminding police of that fact.

"How is the investigation going? Are you working on it? Any new leads?" That was how Bev greeted Hamilton Police Chief Brian Mullan when she saw him in the grocery store on occasion.

The first week in March, a benefit for the Rozendals was held. Five hundred people showed: family, friends, police officers. They had raffles, draws. The money raised went toward an education trust fund for Neil and Jordan. The Rozendal boys also decided to donate some of the money to victims of crime.

Some people who never even knew Art dropped by. One guy donated an electric guitar to the raffle. "It's a testament to the kind of person he was," Art's brother-in-law, Chris Seraphin, said in a *Hamilton Spectator* story. "If we could all have this many friends, we'd be in great shape."

While the Rozendals waited for the police to catch the other attackers and tried to adjust to life without Art, Cory McLeod continued to wait in his cell in Maplehurst Correctional Complex in Milton. He knew how it all worked; knew his DNA profile was on file with police from previous convictions, and knew that if Hamilton police found his DNA at O'Gradys, they could match it to him. And yet, all this time had passed since that night, January 14, almost two months, and he had heard nothing from the cops.

He waited for his next court date on the Kitchener assault charge, certain that he could get a speedy trial, be found innocent. Then he could leave town, perhaps the country. Cory had had no contact with Kyro Sparks since Kyro's arrest. No letters, calls. He knew that was not wise. But Sherri, that was a different matter. He loved that girl. He opened one of her letters:

> March 6, 2005
> Cory, Hey how are you doing? Hey, I'm all right still. I'm in a good mood actually cause I got to talk to you three times today.... I miss you so much....
> I can't wait till we get to be together again, I just never want to be taken away for this long ever again ...

> March 8, 2005
> I don't like that I can only get to talk to you over the phone, and when I go see you, I can only see you through glass....
> You asked me why I hooked up with you, well here's why.
> You are an amazing person, you are sweet, nice, you make me laugh, I feel so comfortable around you....
> Holla back.
> One love.
> Ur wife, Sherri Price
> P.S. Are we still engaged or were u joking around?

Just after 6:00 p.m. on Tuesday, March 8, Mike Maloney took a call from Alexandra Welsh at CFS. She had more results from the testing of the running shoes. She had developed a DNA profile from the insole of the left shoe. The profile indicated that the shoe had been worn by Cory McLeod. The next morning, at 7:30, Sherri's mother heard a knock at the door. She opened it and looked up into the square-jawed face of Detective Greg Jackson. Behind him were several uniformed Waterloo police officers.

"We're here to arrest Sherri Foreman for accessory after the fact of murder," Jackson said. "We have a search warrant for your house."

At that moment, Sherri walked down the stairs. Jackson looked at her. *We're back,* he thought to himself with satisfaction. Her mother looked pretty surprised; so did Sherri, although she wasn't crying or anything. Two officers searched the house. They found letters written between Cory and Sherri. At the same time, Mike Maloney showed up at the door of Katrina McLennan's parents. Katrina, girlfriend of Kyro Sparks, was arrested on the same charge. The girls were each driven to Hamilton. There, Maloney sat with Katrina in an interview room.

"My lawyer advised me not to say anything," she said.

"That's good advice," Maloney replied. "Unfortunately, your lawyer is not the one sitting in the seat here.... What do you think is going to happen to you? You're smiling."

"I'm not."

"This is a serious offence. That man was a lovely guy, had a wife and two children. The whole community of Hamilton loved him."

Maloney showed Katrina a photo of Art's bruised face and asked about Sparks. "There he is; there is the result of your friends beating him.... You think Kyro's worth throwing your life away on?"

"My lawyer advised me not to say anything."

It went on like this — Katrina saying little. "Is there going to be a time when you tell the truth about this? What are you thinking about Katrina?"

"The stain on my pants."

"The stain on your pants."

"Uh-huh."

"Anything else?"

"No."

Hamilton Police Service.

A drawing found in Cory McLeod's notebook.

At the same time, Jackson questioned Sherri in a separate room. "Do you know anyone by the name of Daymein P?"

Sherri said nothing.

"It's a simple yes or no answer. Do you know anyone by the name of Daymein P?"

"I won't say anything. I'm not answering nothing."

"We found papers in your room with Daymein P. written all over them. I'm going to suggest to you that Daymein P. is Cory McLeod. Is that right?"

"I'm not answering nothing. I told you."

Maloney showed her a photo of the Nike shoe found in the garbage. "Whose shoe is that?" he asked.

"Next," she replied. "Next picture."

"Whose shoe is that?"

"Next picture."

The questioning for each girl took just over an hour. The detectives got nowhere. Katrina and Sherri were taken to the lockup. An undercover female officer sat in a cell between them, listening. The girls said little. Sherri was overheard saying: "You guys threw shoes in the garbage?"

That afternoon in the forensic identification department, detectives Gary Zwicker and Annette Huys examined the papers found in Sherri's room. Huys had heard how the interrogations had gone. She was astounded by the girls' behaviour. Teenagers, in the middle of a murder investigation, and they didn't budge. Standing by their man, she reflected sardonically.

She studied a sketchbook of drawings by Cory McLeod. Buried in among his doodles she noticed a stick figure drawing. It depicted three figures, wearing crowns, who appeared to be stomping on a fourth, who did not wear a crown. Her eyes lit up. Waterloo Police had said McLeod and Sparks were members of a Kitchener gang called the Kings.

The morning arrests of Katrina and Sherri were just phase one on arrest day. Peter Abi-Rashed had developed an operational plan assigning 17 Hamilton officers and three from Waterloo to make arrests and search residences.

At 3:15 p.m. that day, Cory McLeod was led by a jail official into an interview room at Maplehurst. In through another door walked two men in suits. Maloney and Jackson.

"Cory McLeod," Maloney said, "you are under arrest for murder in the second degree of Arthur Rozendal in Hamilton on January 14, 2005."

Jackson read him his rights, then he was cuffed and taken back to Hamilton. Among his personal items were a pair of white Nike shoes that had "Kings" and "D.P" written on them. In the Major Crime Unit, he was led through a room where the detectives had posted investigation photos, maps, diagrams. It was tactical — give the accused a sense of what they have. Shock him. *We already know it all, you might as well talk.*

Cory was shaken by what he saw. There were autopsy photos on the wall. He had never seen anything like it. The images stayed in his mind's eye; he could not shake them. Still, while taken aback by the display, and surprised at how quickly the police had gathered so much evidence against him, Cory was not about to talk. He knew the drill.

At 8:00 p.m. Maloney began the interrogation. "Back on January 14, when this happened, were you living in Hamilton or Kitchener?" he asked.

"I don't have anything to say about any of these things. I don't know what you're talking about."

"Anything regarding the homicide type of thing?"

"Yeah."

"You are in way over your head."

"Yeah, I know."

"Sometimes we come in here and tap dance and try to trick you into giving a statement, but you know what? We have so much evidence against you I don't have to do that.... I see you have a tattoo on your wrist. The Kings. Is that some street gang?"

"No, it's not a gang."

"What is 'the Kings'?"

"I think I'm a king."

"Do you?"

"Yeah."

"I see you have DP on your shoe. What does that mean?"

"It's personal."

Maloney held up a photocopy of the crown-wearing stick figures doodle from Cory's sketchbook.

"I'm wondering, Cory, if that's you and your two Kings gang buddies stomping someone. Because if that's a fact, then it's first degree murder."

"That's doodling."

"Done by you. Just so happens our murder, January 14, there were three males who stomped a guy to death. Just coincidence?"

"Yeah."

After Maloney, Greg Jackson entered and continued the questions. Cory refused to answer. Didn't do anything to anybody, he claimed. No comment on whether he was Daymein P.

Cory waited for the one playing bad cop. Just after midnight, he arrived. After the cool manner of Jackson and Maloney, Abi-Rashed entered the room like a brewing storm.

"Cory," he said. "Cory, Cory, Cory. I'm their boss. You got nothing to say, right?"

"Yeah. I'm done talking."

"You're done talking?"

Abi-Rashed chuckled, then sat quietly, tapping his thick fingers on the table. "How are the sandwiches? Cheese. No ham? What shall we talk about? How you're going away for a long time? When's the last time you kissed Sherri? On the 14th or 15th? You know that's the last time you will kiss her, right? You know what second-degree murder is? Life. The more I listen to you saying, 'I got nothing to say, I didn't have anything to do with it,' the more I get excited, because that's what I want you to repeat."

He held up a photo of Art and his family. "Look at the picture of a nice family with two teenagers, a wife. Nice man, never hurt anybody. And who's behind his death? Cory. Right?"

He said nothing.

"We have been going, 'You know what? I don't think we need to work on this case anymore because Cory is done like dinner.' The victim's blood is on your shoes. You do the math, Cory. We got your chain, we got Daymein P.; your girlfriend calls you that. We got your DNA. You were there, Cory."

"I don't even know what you're talking about."

"Good one! That's what I wanna hear. 'I don't know what you're talking about.' The more you say that, the better it is for me, because every time you say it, it's a lie. You've been lying all night.... I want to thank you for making this a pretty easy case for us. Thanks buddy. Hang tight eh?"

Cory McLeod was locked up downstairs.

The next day Mike Maloney and another officer sat with him. Maloney told Cory they needed to take a fresh DNA sample. His profile existed on a national database but by the book they were required to do another. If he refused to give a sample, Maloney said, they could use any amount of force necessary to get it.

"What, you and him?" Cory said, motioning to the other officer in the room. Maloney grinned. Gang punks think they're tough, but only fight when they have weapons or outnumber a victim.

"No, Cory. Actually, if it comes to that I'll ask him to leave," Maloney said.

12

"HE DESERVES TO DIE"

On Thursday, March 17, at 3:30 p.m., Maloney, Jackson, and Abi-Rashed met at the station with an officer from Peel Region. The officer had been contacted by a registered paid informant about the Rozendal homicide. The informant had insisted on remaining anonymous, and would not testify in court. He had a solid pipeline to Sparks and McLeod. Through the Peel officer, the informant said the chain and dog tag were Cory's, and Daymein P. meant that "if you deal with the devil, you will pay a price."

He described what happened at O'Grady's. Art had tried to play peacemaker. He had put his hand on Kyro in the bathroom, Kyro lost it on Art, and Cory had joined in and jumped up and down on Art's back. Kyro, Cory, and a third guy who had been with them fled the bar to the girls' apartment. There, Kyro was still upset with Cory, which is why he headed outside, leading to his arrest. Cory told Sherri to wash his clothes and throw out his shoes.

What about the third guy? the police asked. The informant said he knew who it was, but would not give the name. "You'll never figure out who the third person is," he had told his police contact.

Paid informants usually showed the police they had quality information, gave them a nibble, then held out for more money in exchange for critical details. The informant wanted $5,000 for the third guy's name. Hamilton Police paid him $4,000.

Sunday night at 9:00 p.m., the phone rang at Maloney's home. It was the Peel officer. The informant had more. Maloney took notes as the officer relayed the message. The third guy involved came into Hamilton from Kitchener the night of the murder and left the next morning; Kyro, Cory, and the third guy talked at Katrina's apartment soon after the assault.

Cory said: "I think we killed the guy."

The third guy said: "No, I saw him moving."

Kyro added: "I don't give a fuck. Fuck him. He touched me he deserves to die."

The informant had provided the name of the third guy. Maloney wrote it down. He was from Kitchener, was close to Sparks and McLeod. He had been 17 years old at the time of the homicide, so fell under the Youth Criminal Justice Act. That meant police could not publicly release his name. But he could still be charged with murder. And that was what Maloney intended to do.

He ordered surveillance on the youth. A plainclothes officer would follow him to obtain a cast-off or "goop sample" for DNA analysis — the police would wait for him to spit or blow his nose, then they would retrieve and package for evidence.

On March 29 the surveillance unit spotted the youth and collected spit he left on a Kitchener sidewalk. The sample was bagged. On April 19 Maloney took a call from CFS. The cast-off sample matched the DNA from a drinking straw at O'Grady's the night of the homicide. On May 12 Maloney and Jackson drove to Waterloo to arrest him. He was in high school that day. At 1:00 p.m. they met him in the school office.

"We are detectives from Hamilton," Maloney told him. "I guess that's not good news for you."

The youth said nothing.

"You are under arrest for the murder of Arthur Rozendal. Do you wish to say anything in answer to the charge?"

"No."

The preliminary hearing into the second degree murder charges against Kyro Sparks, Cory McLeod, and the youth was slated to begin in October. Assistant Crown attorney Joe Nadel had been tapped to handle the case. Nadel, 55, had a reputation as a relentless prosecutor. The detectives continued to follow up on tips, waited on more forensic results, and the final post-mortem report from the forensic pathologist — which included a microscopic study of Art's brain.

On April 21 Alex Welsh contacted Maloney. The biology section at CFS had worked on the Daymein P. chain for two months, breaking the chain and dog tags into sections, trying to develop DNA profiles for two individuals. The final result? A profile of Cory McLeod's DNA had been discovered on the chain. Not much surprise there. But there was another DNA profile developed from the chain as well: Art Rozendal's. Before he died, Art had clearly struggled, grabbed Cory's chain in the fight — and left a clue for the police. *Another nail in the coffin*, Maloney thought.

"The signs of blunt force trauma to Mr. Rozendal's body — are those injuries a significant contributing cause to his death?"

"Yes," replied Dr. John Fernandes.

The preliminary hearing at John Sopinka Courthouse in Hamilton was underway. The forensic pathologist answered questions on the stand from assistant Crown attorney Joe Nadel. The hearing before Justice Richard Jennis would determine whether the case made it through to a second-degree murder trial. A key issue was the cause of death.

Fernandes had signed off on his post-mortem report on September 7, concluding that the cause of death was "blunt force trauma to the head, neck. and chest. and evidence of chest compression" as a consequence of "stomping while under the influence of alcohol." That was not what Mike Maloney wanted to hear. To prove murder in court, it was better to have an unequivocal cause of death — blunt force trauma, period, without contributing injuries and other factors like alcohol consumption to muddy the waters.

Defence lawyer Edward Sapiano cross-examined Fernandes.

"Let me ask you this: Could one sustain two kicks to the head and not die?"

"Yes."

"In fact, one could sustain 10 kicks to the head and not die, correct?"

"Yes."

Art died when his heart stopped, which was in part caused by a lack of oxygen to the brain. The alcohol level in his blood was 234 milligrams per 100 ml of blood. (Art was not driving that night, but by comparison, the legal limit is 80 mg/100 ml.)

"Diluted blood carries less oxygen, correct?" Sapiano asked.

"Yes."

"So to the extent there was alcohol in Mr. Rozendal's system, given the lack of oxygen to the brain, the alcohol played a role?"

"Yes."

"Given what we have seen here in terms of the manifest injuries," Sapiano said, "I'm going to suggest that Mr. Rozendal's demise was not something that was readily predictable."

"If I beat you — if I beat you enough — I think most people would expect that, yes, some of those injuries could kill you," Fernandes replied.

The Crown called nearly 20 witnesses to the hearing, to re-create the night Art died and paint a picture of the evidence pointing at Kyro Sparks, Cory McLeod, and the youth as his killers. Through it all, week after week, Brenda Rozendal sat in the hallway outside court. She was not permitted inside because she would be called as a witness if the case went to trial. The police had gathered layers of evidence. But did they have enough for a murder conviction? Standard procedure was to set the bar high in every homicide investigation — first degree murder — then work from that. But Maloney knew things changed when the results of an investigation started to pass through the legal system.

On October 13 Maloney and investigators Greg Jackson and Peter Abi-Rashed met with prosecutor, Joe Nadel. Four days after that, they met with Brenda and her family. They had some bad news. The charges against the third guy, the youth, were being dropped. They had enough evidence to get the youth committed to stand trial with Sparks and McLeod, but the Crown felt there wasn't sufficient evidence to get a conviction. Eyewitnesses and DNA put the youth in the bar and in the back hallway, but no direct evidence had been uncovered that he had hit Art.

Maloney and Jackson visited a youth detention centre where he had been held since they arrested him.

"We got some good news and some bad news," Maloney told him. "The good news is, you're getting out. The bad news is, we're serving you with a subpoena to testify."

On November 4 he took the stand at the preliminary hearing.

"Would you like to see Mr. McLeod convicted or acquitted of the murder of Arthur Rozendal?" Nadel asked.

"Acquitted."

"Would you like to see Mr. Sparks convicted or acquitted of that crime?"

"Acquitted."

"Do you know of a crew in Kitchener called the Kings?"

"Yes."

"Are you a member of that crew?"

"No."

"What about Mr. McLeod, is he a member?"

"I don't know."

"What about Mr. Sparks?"

"I don't know."

He admitted to being in O'Grady's the night of the homicide. He then offered an entirely different version of events in the bar. He said that there was a fourth guy with them, someone he had never seen before. Said that this other guy had gotten in an "argument" with Art in the hallway, punched and kicked him. Then Kyro and Cory had happened on the scene. Going on, the youth told Nadel that Cory tripped over Art and then they see him on the floor. According to the youth, when they saw Art lying on the floor they had "puzzled looks on their faces."

Kyro then "nudged him with his foot to see if he was all right" and said, "Yo, are you all right man?"

Jackson sat in court trying to hold back a smirk of disdain. A joke. Nothing but a joke. The story ran contrary to all of the eyewitness and forensic evidence. Clearly, the youth was lying, protecting the other two. His testimony was worthless. Neither the Crown, nor surely even the defence, would bother calling him to take the stand down the road; nobody would believe a word of it. The youth was now out of the picture, although Maloney kept him in the rear-view mirror. If someone spilled more information down the road about his role in Art's death, they could still bring a fresh charge against him. Maloney requested a photo lineup with the youth in it for future reference.

The preliminary hearing ended on November 7. On December 13 the judge made his ruling: Kyro Sparks and Cory McLeod would stand trial for second-degree murder.

And then, eight months later, everything changed.

On August 23 Brenda, Art's mom, Frances, and other family met at the Crown attorney's office with, among others, Nadel and Maloney. The family was told the news. Sparks and McLeod wanted a plea deal. They would, finally, admit that they beat Art — in exchange for the Crown downgrading their charge from second-degree murder to manslaughter. Nadel wanted to sign. Brenda was angry, but not with the Crown or the detectives. She wanted the maximum penalty, wanted the murder charge to stick on the killers for what they did to Art. Maloney had prepared her for the possibility the charge could change. In fact he had had a gnawing feeling since he first worked on the homicide that, no matter how solid a case they built, with an apparently random homicide like this one, it might end this way.

He knew one weakness of their murder case was the relatively ambiguous cause of death. The other, was proving intent. Sparks and McLeod had never met Art before. There was no suggestion of premeditation. After the homicide they had walked from O'Grady's, as though being unaware that had Art died. Kyro had hung around in the area afterward. A jury might be convinced that they had not acted like murderers after the crime.

Cory's drawing of the three kings could have been used to show that he had celebrated a murder — except he claimed he had drawn the sketch long before the beating. Their paid informant had quoted Kyro saying that Art "deserves to die" — but that could not be raised in court because the informant refused to testify. And Sherri Foreman and Katrina McLennan had revealed nothing about what their boyfriends said after the homicide. Brenda agreed with the Crown. She didn't want to risk the killers walking free.

"Take the deal," she told them. "Put them behind bars."

The Crown officially accepted the deal in court on August 25. At the sentencing hearing on November 2, 2006, at John Sopinka Courthouse, Brenda stood and read her victim impact statement. The judge, Justice James Kent, would consider the information in handing down the sentence. She talked about her pain missing Art, and the difficulty of living with her sense of safety for her family ripped apart. Brenda's sister, Bev, also spoke, as did Art's sister, Debbie.

Neil, their eldest son, took the stand, felt himself shaking. He didn't have to speak, but was determined to stare down his dad's killers. Neil talked about how much he loved his dad, how much it hurt with him gone. He barely looked at the pages as he looked into the faces of Sparks and McLeod. When he finished Neil stepped down and gave the finger to the killers. He kept going out the door. He entered a bathroom, threw up, and wept.

Assistant Crown attorney Tony Leitch argued for 15-year sentences. The defence argued for seven to eight. On November 3 the judge ruled: 11 years, less time served. It wasn't the maximum. Brenda tried to keep reminding herself that they also could have received less. At least they would do hard time. And then something unusual happened.

After the killers were led from the courtroom in shackles, Brenda and her family gathered, then moved across the aisle and met with Cory McLeod's parents. (Kyro Sparks had no family in court.) The two families exchanged handshakes and hugs and shed tears. There was Art's family, showing empathy for the killer's family. Nobody who worked in a court-room had ever seen anything like it. A nice moment, Mike Maloney re-flected, but then the warm feelings did not last.

The sentence was yet another in a string of homicide cases that had left the detective with a bitter taste in his mouth. Hamilton: the man-slaughter capital of Canada, he vented. He knew that, given the evidence on the table, manslaughter was probably the most they could get. But those two guys didn't get enough time. You could never get enough for taking a person's life, he felt. Maloney lamented that he worked in a legal system, not a justice system. He was tired of apologizing to families about how it worked.

13

WINDING ROADS

Cory McLeod fears his dreams, and so stays up late each night in his cell, till 2:30, 3:00 a.m. — it allows him to drift into the kind of unconscious sleep where images of his past do not visit. It's the things he has seen — the graphic photos of Art Rozendal the police showed him among them. When he does dream, sometimes it is of that night at O'Grady's. Except sometimes it plays out differently; he and Kyro don't beat up Art. Or Art even beats on them. Or nothing happens between them at all.

In Millhaven, a maximum security prison near Kingston, Ontario, Cory has a prayer mat in his cell, says he has found religion, is a practising Muslim. He speaks quickly, is animated. He expresses remorse for what happened; believes he and Kyro deserve every punishment they got, if not more. He lives in J-unit, where Canada's hardest criminals are kept. The way Cory sees it, he can use his time in jail to change who he is. In a way, he thinks, somebody lost their life so he can better his, even if that "might seem a fucked-up way to look at it." He feels he owes it to the Rozendals to turn his life around.

Does Cory mean what he says? Is he just playing another game? If so, to what end? He sees Kyro in jail regularly; they are on the same security range. They are still close friends. Workout at the same time with weights. Not together, though. They can't agree on the routines. Cory still loves Sherri Foreman, was shocked she did that for him, stonewalled the police. He is proud, in a way, but also wishes she hadn't done it. If she had co-operated with police, they could still be in touch today. As it is, Sherri is legally prohibited from any contact with him.

In February 2007 Sherri Foreman and Katrina McLennan pleaded guilty and were convicted for obstructing police. The judge said the girls had been "attracted to the gang lifestyle." Their conduct "struck at the heart of the administration of justice," and "showed a lack of respect for human life and a lack of respect for the people of Hamilton." Due to the timing of their bail hearings, Sherri ended up spending 50 days in jail, Katrina 23. The judge sentenced them to time served and three years' probation. They must stay out of Hamilton and have no contact with Sparks or McLeod.

Kyro Sparks? He wears a white Nike hat perched sideways on his head, the price tag still attached. Unlike Cory he speaks guardedly, measuring his words. Won't talk about the homicide, or his version of what happened in the bathroom.

"I'd like to talk about it," he offers, "but not until I talk to my co-accused."

Why did he beat up Art?

"I'll decline to answer that question."

Does he wish Art had not died that night?

"I don't wish death on nobody, not even my worst enemies."

Does he feel the Rozendal family's pain, having lost a father and husband?

"Do I feel their pain?" he repeats, a puzzled look on his face.

He looks away in thought for several seconds. Before he can form an answer, a guard comes and takes him back to his cell, the thick black steel door automatically clanking into place behind him.

Art's old friend from work, Charlie Montgomery, drove up the Mountain to visit Brenda. He had some things to give her. In the coke ovens at Stelco, Art's locker had remained untouched long after he died; inside were his tools, his clothes — and the tarnished helmet that hung from a hook on the wall. None of the guys could bring themselves to touch any of it, least of all Art's supervisor, Ken, a guy who wore his heart on his sleeve. Finally, Charlie decided that it was time. So on an August day, two and a half years after Art was killed, when Charlie pulled up Brenda's street, Art's clothes were in the back of his car. He had carefully set the helmet on the front passenger seat. Felt good to hand the helmet over. Art's boys should have it.

Art's oldest son, Neil, talks openly about his father's death and the effect it has had on him and his family. It helps him to deal with his loss. He talks, to a journalist, family, about his dad, the pain. That's his way. Jordan, who is quieter, keeps to himself, says little. He inherited Art's mechanical abilities. Eventually, Jordan found his way into Art's garage, the one that still has the girlie tool calendars, a collection of dented licence plates — and a '68 buttercup-yellow Buick GS 400. Art had taken it apart, the engine sits on the floor. Never did finish it. Jordan took over the project.

The day Charlie Montgomery came out, Brenda held a backyard barbecue for a few friends and family. A good time, but then it seemed to collectively hit everyone at once. Brenda had bought these great steaks. But who would cook? Anyone can grill a steak, but nobody did it like Art. He had his special marinade, and the way he seared them locked in the flavour. Everyone just stood there, staring at the empty barbecue, and that's when it occurred to Charlie. The family is still living with Art. Except he's not here.

On the third anniversary of Art's death, Brenda awoke early with tears in her eyes. The morning broke grey, shrouded in fog. She drove with Neil and Jordan to Woodland Cemetery. They gathered at Art's plot and held hands. Bev had put a little angel figure there. Inset in the stone is a picture of a red '71 Buick Skylark, the first one Art got Brenda. On the stone Brenda had a quote inscribed: "The love we shared will never die."

Like every time she visits, she laid three single roses. The yellow rose symbolizes friendship, the white symbolizes purity, and the red, love. Then Art's wife and two sons left, drove over a wooden bridge crossing an inlet of the lake that bends into the property, where Art and Brenda had once posed for their wedding photos.

Brenda visited the cemetery every day for about a year after he died. Then it was probably once a month, when she had the day off from her work in home health care. She keeps busy with the boys, work, friends, family, and volunteering with Hamilton Police Victim Services, where she helps counsel loved ones of homicide victims. She misses Art every day, but also fears forgetting too much, worrying that with time he will fade. What did he sound like? What did he smell like?

She worries that the strongest memory lodged in her mind's eye is not the smile and laughter, but Art dying in O'Grady's. She swears she can still taste his blood on her tongue, and no amount of cigarettes can make it go away.

On that anniversary of his death, the fog cleared, the wind picked up; the air was bitterly cold. She drove with the boys up Upper James Street to the bar. It's not called O'Grady's Roadhouse anymore. Neil wanted to go. He drops in the bar once a year by himself; Brenda doesn't like him doing it. Today, she didn't want to go, but went to be with him. Jordan remained in the van with a friend of his. It was quiet inside the bar: two, maybe three people, middle of the afternoon, sports on TV. Brenda and Neil sat near where their old table had been. A waitress came over. "Can I get you a drink?" They ordered two Canadians.

"To Art," she said, her voice shaking. Neil stared at the spot at the bar where he had last seen his dad alive. Then he stood and walked to the back hallway. There was no longer a door concealing the back; you could see right through to the bathroom area. Brenda looked over her shoulder at Neil. Her hands shook, just a bit, and her eyes looked glassy.

She had done this once before, last year; came to the bar to confront the demons. And here she was doing it again, as though forcing herself to feel pain, because even the pain of remembering how he left her was better than not feeling him at all. Neil punched in music on the juke box. One of Art's favourites: "Wonderwall" by Oasis.

And all the roads we have to walk along are winding
And all the lights that lead us there are blinding

Before Brenda and Neil were ready to leave, Jordan entered through the front door. The family was in the place all of 20 minutes. Brenda and the boys walked to the back hallway, stood, bowed their heads for a moment. Then the three of them turned and walked out the front door.

Art's younger brother Darren moved back to Hamilton and got a place in the north end; found work dealing with heating and cooling systems,

John Rennison, *Hamilton Spectator.*

Art's brother, Darren, struggled to cope with his anger.

duct work. He is around Brenda's place nearly every day, helping out with the boys, fixing stuff.

He is not coping. It's not just the grief, which is constant. He thinks of Art every day. When Art died Darren lost a brother and father figure on the same day. He just misses having him around. More than grief, though, he feels anger. It will not leave. The thing is, he knows Art would actually have had it in his heart to forgive the ones who killed him. He really would. Art was just like his mom, had strong faith. Darren? Forgive? No. Truth is, he'd like an hour in a room alone with each of those guys. Eye for an eye. It's in the Bible. He knows Art would tell him, "Darren, you have to forgive. Have to move on. Don't think about the past." But see, Art's not here to say it. Because they took him away.

Some of Art's gifts, though, nobody can take away. Darren has seen Art in a dream — just once. In the dream Darren is sleeping and is awakened by the sound of a voice. He peers across the darkened room, and there is Art, sitting up in his own bed, looking at him. The voice is quiet. "Come here," Art says. Darren rises, shuffles over and kneels. Art leans in and hugs his brother, holds him tight. The grip loosens and Darren gently lays Art back down again.

Brenda Rozendal recently sold the house she had shared with Art and her sons. She has done volunteer work with Hamilton Police Victim Services, helping others who face traumatic loss.

Mike Maloney retired after 32 years and eight months with a badge. He says he never thinks about Sparks and McLeod, but still thinks about the Rozendals and other families coping with incomplete justice, and is still in touch with some of them, including Brenda. He golfs a few times a week with a couple of retired cops. His shots don't always fly straight but they fly straight enough, and the beer after the round is always cold: "It's just nice to be out there. Being a police officer taught me that life is fragile and fleeting — enjoy while you can."

Kyro Sparks and Cory McLeod became eligible for early release in the fall of 2012. January 2013 will be the eighth anniversary of Art's death. Art would have turned 52 in February 2013.

MORE TRUE CRIME BOOKS FROM DUNDURN

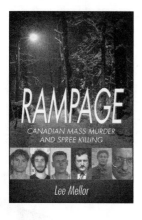

Rampage
Canadian Mass Murder and Spree Killing
by Lee Mellor
978-1459707214
$21.99

Lee Mellor gathers dozens of Canada's most lethal mass and spree killers into a single work, including such notorious mass murderers as Marc Lépine and Peter John Peters. *Rampage* details their grisly crimes, delves into their twisted psyches, and dissects their motivations to answer the question every true crime lover yearns to know: why?

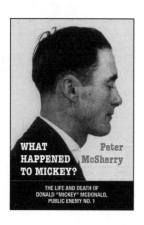

What Happened to Mickey?
The Life and Death of Donald "Mickey" McDonald, Public Enemy No. 1
by Peter McSherry
978-1459707382
$24.99

Until the age of 31, Donald McDonald was only "dirty little Mickey from 'The Corner,'" the notorious intersection of Toronto's Jarvis and Dundas Streets in a neighbourhood known in the 1930s as "Gangland." After Mickey was charged with the January 1939 murder of bookmaker Jimmy Windsor, he became a national crime figure. What followed were two murder trials, a liquor-truck hijacking, a sensational three-man escape in 1947 from Kingston Penitentiary, and a $50,000 bank robbery.

DUNDURN
www.dundurn.com